New Mexico Past and Future

∞

N·E·W
M·E·X·I·C·O
Past and Future

Thomas E. Chávez

UNIVERSITY OF NEW MEXICO PRESS ∞ ALBUQUERQUE

LIBRARY OF CONGRESS CATALOGING-IN-PUBLICATION DATA

Chávez, Thomas E.
New Mexico past and future / Thomas E. Chávez.
p. cm.
Includes bibliographical references and index.
ISBN-13: 978-0-8263-3444-2 (PBK. : ALK. PAPER)
ISBN-10: 0-8263-3444-X (PBK. : ALK. PAPER)
1. New Mexico—History. I. Title.
F796.C44 2006
978.9—dc22

2006017806

∞

Book and cover design
and type composition: Kathleen Sparkes
This book was typeset using Minion 11.5/13.5; 26P
Display type is Incognito and Latino Elongated

Dedicated to

Dr. Myra Ellen Jenkins,

who made history, and

Dr. Celia López Chávez,

who is making history

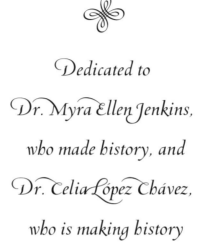

Contents

ভ৫

List of Illustrations

⚜

Acknowledgments

෧෬

While my name appears on the cover and spine of this book, I by no means can take sole credit for the book's publication. The history alone is a culmination of hundreds of historians who have shared the product of their research and knowledge. The critiques of Dr. Richard Ellis of Fort Lewis College; Dr. Vern Scarborough of the University of Cincinnati; Dr. Nasario Garcia, retired from New Mexico Highlands University; Dr. Paul Kraemer, retired from the Los Alamos Laboratory; and my father, Judge Antonio E. Chávez, also retired, helped me to transmit that history into a readable whole. Sarah Pilcher Ritthaler's final edit polished the manuscript into its final product.

The organization of the book with its illustrations and vignettes interspersed throughout evolved out of an earlier book of mine titled *An Illustrated History of New Mexico*. That book depended on quotes and images from the past. Dr. Richard Rudisill, a former colleague and, in many ways, mentor, gave me the idea for that book's concept. He deserves credit for planting the seed out of which grew the organizational concept for this book.

The staff at the University of New Mexico Press, including Lisa Pacheco and Kathy Sparkes, enthusiastically embraced the idea of this book to design a handsome and, I believe, intriguing publication.

My friend and coworker at the Palace of the Governors, Blair Clark, took the photograph on the front cover. The photograph is of the Juan Martínez de Montoya documents that the staff, supporters, and I rediscovered and secured for New Mexico. The documents were lost in private ownership in London, England, and now are housed in the Fray Angélico Chávez History Library at the Palace of the Governors. The bound documents are open to one of the two places were Martínez de Montoya, a captain under Juan de Oñate from 1601 until 1609, testified that he had founded Santa Fe. It reads, "y el haber hecho plaza de Santa Fe," "and the fact that having made the plaza of Santa Fe."

The idea of writing this history of New Mexico in an essay format came from Luther Wilson, the director of UNM Press. Never the man to let a good idea languish, he then encouraged me to undertake the task.

At once honored that I would be approached for the book and intimidated at the idea of doing it, I accepted the challenge. I could not help but draw an analogy from yesteryear's composers of classical music who wrote in various formats such as symphonies, cantatas, and operas. Once completed, their music was compared to the music of other composers done in the same format. So, it seemed to me that I had been asked to write a history that other very good historians had written and, undoubtedly, will write in the future. This history of New Mexico would be my cantata and like those composers who many times had been retained to create their works, I, too, had been honored—selected out of many very good historians of New Mexico to write this story.

Thus, while I, by no means, would consider myself better than my past and present colleagues, I hope that this history will stand with theirs and in some ways do them homage.

That I chose Dr. Myra Ellen Jenkins to share the dedication of this book will make sense to any student of New Mexico. She was a friend and colleague, and is always an inspiration, who coauthored one of those earlier histories of New Mexico. Dr. Jenkins shares the dedication with another historian, Dr. Celia López-Chávez, who is my wife and teaches Latin American topics in the University Honors Program at the University of New Mexico. She is making history today, helped with this book, and had the privilege of becoming a friend of Dr. Jenkins before the latter's death. As much as anybody, this history is theirs.

The Department of History at UNM, where I attended graduate school, took my curiosity and showed me how to become a historian. We career historians sometimes forget or overlook the flame kindled by our graduate professors. My chairman was Dr. Donald Cutter, who taught a wonderful history of New Mexico, another early source for this book. Then there is the family and friends without whom nothing is possible. My historian uncle, Fray Angélico Chávez, encouraged me in ways I will never know. My daughters, Nicolasa Marie, herself a historian working in museums, and her departed younger sister, Christel Angélica, along with my parents, Marilyn S. Chávez and Antonio E. Chávez, my brother, sisters, and aunts and uncles, especially Allen Sprowl, who is more like a brother, are the real reason for this and all my books, for I want to make them proud. Hopefully subsequent generations will be as affected.

Introduction

☙❧

The history of a place can be approached in many ways. The story can be narrative, conceptual from a point of view—theoretical, etc. New Mexico's wondrous history is no exception. Yet, because the majority of New Mexico's history is filled with non-English-speaking peoples with their customs, mores, languages, and lifestyles, many casual students have found the subject daunting if not downright confusing.

New Mexico was not always called New Mexico. Thousands of years of human history occurred in the area before the first documented mention by a Franciscan friar in 1571 of "La Nueva México," meaning "Another Mexico," in reference to Mexico City. That other Mexico was a landlocked area that would expand and shrink over the next four plus centuries. Always though, the area extended from "the pass," El Paso del Norte, north to where the Pueblo Indians lived. The Rio Grande, or Rio Bravo del Norte, running in a north-to-south corridor in the middle of the area, would become the primary topographical as well as life-sustaining feature. With exceptions, New Mexico is mountainous to the north and west with high plains and desert to the east, northwest, and south. It is an arid land, cut by mesas, tablelands, and canyons. While none of the mountainous peaks are snow-clad year-round, they do receive heavy winter snowpacks that help replenish the Rio Grande, Pecos, San Juan, Chama, and Gila rivers. The air is clear, the light is bright, and people can see great distances, giving the scenery, while not colorful, a sense of grandeur.

Significantly, natural barriers form none of New Mexico's borders. There are no oceans or even great rivers upon which ocean-going vessels can navigate. New Mexico is landlocked and to most people who are from elsewhere, the area can easily appear, as one of its early Spanish governors described it, "remote beyond compare."

For purposes of simplicity, if not clarity, this approach to New Mexico's history will be in chronological form with an epilogue sharing some of the author's conceptual ideas. The chronological narrative will be in broad strokes in an attempt to get the reader to "see the forest for the trees."

This history is an attempt to provide the general public with an updated, handy, and functional narrative of New Mexico's past. The idea is not new. The very reason for this book is that the University of New Mexico Press published *A Brief History of New Mexico*, coauthored by two of New Mexico's excellent scholars, the late Myra Ellen Jenkins, a historian, and Albert Schroeder, an ethnohistorian and archaeologist. This 1974 publication proved invaluable and, indeed, timeless. The book became immensely popular and useful. It more than fulfilled the expectations of the New Mexico Cultural Property Review Committee, which had the vision to have the book published. The committee, made up of an astounding array of New Mexico's historians, preservationists, and archaeologists, first issued a two-volume report titled *The Historic Preservation Program for New Mexico* in 1973. Jenkins and Schroeder's book was a reprint of a portion of volume I.

Of course, there were other histories of New Mexico. Most students of my generation, if they took a New Mexico history course in one of the state's universities, are familiar with Warren A. Beck's *New Mexico: A History of Four Centuries*. Preeminent historian Marc Simmons published his history of the state, *New Mexico: An Interpretive History*, for the national bicentennial commission in 1976. Simmons's book is my personal favorite.

But time has passed and new generations have added to the body of historical knowledge. New discoveries have been made, new information has been shared, and new documents, indeed collections of documents, have surfaced. All of this points to the need to update the seminal work of Jenkins and Schroeder. The original idea behind this book was to create another "brief" history. That idea died quickly. "Brief" was eliminated and the project to create a new history evolved to the point where it became a historical essay—kind of a personal impression of New Mexico's heritage and its importance.

The reader should keep in mind two general rules while making sense of a long, complicated history. First, in the grand themes of history, dates and names, while included, are not so important. Relative time, cause and effect, are the important keys to making sense of any history. Nothing happens without a context, nor can it. An event always occurs as a result of its context and many events that preceded it. Naturally enough, that same event will be a cause of many further events that will follow. For example, it is not necessary to know the author's birth date or remember his name to benefit from this book. What is significant is that an individual was born and gained some expertise to write a book *before* he wrote it. Cause and effect is important to the understanding of history.

Second, human history is just that, the story of human beings— people like you and me who laugh and cry, love and hate, feel sadness and happiness and pain, and need to eat and drink to stay alive. They are not figures printed on pages, anonymous phantoms of yesteryear. In this case, they are people who lived in the land that came to be called New Mexico. In this sense, history is fascinating enough that there is no need for fiction because human beings' natural inconsistencies and foibles will provide the student of history with more than enough drama.

New Mexico's historical canvas is divided into five grand sections. First is the period before the Europeans arrived. This period of pre-European contact began some twelve thousand, and possibly more, years ago. Archaeologists and anthropologists do not have the benefit of the written word to study the people of this period, though their art provides a record of sorts. Like writing, art can convey thought processes. For the most part, scholars of this period must investigate the remnants of the material culture left behind by ancient societies to piece together who they were and what they did.

The second period is the Spanish colonial period, which begins with the first European expeditions into the area in 1536. The period ended almost three centuries later when Mexico achieved its independence from Spain in 1821. The Spanish kept written records that, when added to the research of their material culture, give scholars a more detailed picture of their story. A preponderance of information for this and subsequent periods can be found in archives in the United States, Mexico, Spain, and elsewhere.

Mexican independence resulted in the third and shortest period of New Mexico's history. This period lasted until 1846, when the United States declared war on Mexico and the U.S. army occupied New Mexico. Or, the period lasted until 1848, when the Treaty of Guadalupe Hidalgo ended the war and made New Mexico a part of the United States. These transitional years are a curious and turbulent as well as key time of New Mexico's history and still are not understood completely.

The fourth period is called the territorial period, although until 1850 the United States military occupied the area and ran the government. Nevertheless, New Mexico became a United States Territory in 1850 and remained so for the next sixty-two years. Initially, the new territory lost land to Texas and the new state of Colorado. The San Luis Valley went to Colorado. El Paso, considered a part of New Mexico until 1824, became a part of Texas, while the Mesilla Valley, the site of Mesilla and Las Cruces, was in Mexico for a short period. On the other hand, New Mexico's capital, Santa Fe, governed the present state of Arizona as part of its territory until 1863, when Arizona became a new territory.

After a long struggle, New Mexico succeeded in becoming a state in 1912. The statehood period is the fifth and last period of New Mexico's history—at least, so far. This is the period about which we know the most and probably have the most difficulty objectively describing, for it is the period in which we all live and are, in fact, making history. This is a period in which, like Henry Adams's "Virgin and Dynamo" described in the epilogue, New Mexico has maintained its heritage while progressing in the modern world. From statehood until now, society has moved from the horse to space travel, from the telephone to e-mail, and so on. The impact of the modern world on New Mexico's ancient cultures is, to say the least, an interesting study, for the people have used their cultures to survive.

As we strive to fill in and add detail to the five periods of New Mexico's historical canvas, some factual observations should be noted from the beginning. These facts, in and of themselves, should raise questions beyond their intrinsic interest. And these facts speak to the narrative history, perhaps creating a heightened interest as that narrative is read.

New Mexico is the only state in the Union that has "U.S.A." on its automobile license plates. This is not done out of any sense of patriotism. Rather, New Mexicans learned early on that they needed to explain to the rest of the country that New Mexico is one of the fifty states. There still exists a lack of understanding about New Mexico.

New Mexico is the only official bilingual state in the Union. Ballots are printed in Spanish and English, many of the state's major newspapers have sections in Spanish, and there are Spanish newspapers. The state offers driving examinations in Spanish or English. But while Spanish and English are the state's most visible languages, the state's twenty-two Native American tribes and nations maintain their own languages as well, in many cases as the primary language of the community. Beyond word of mouth, many of the state's universities offer courses in Native American languages such as Navajo.

So, the statement that New Mexico is a unique state is not trite. Its history speaks to many cultural differences within the history of the United States, in fact, forcing the larger national history to expand its boundaries to include other peoples, more mother countries, a richer variety of language and customs, and, importantly, a different way of viewing our patrimony.

Beyond that, New Mexico's history contains some lessons for the rest of the world. Hopefully, this book is an introduction to that history and will help bring into focus its profound importance so that it may be shared.

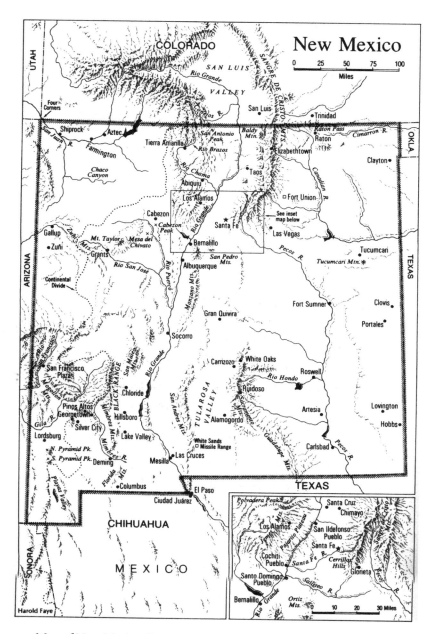

Map of New Mexico. From Marc Simmons, New Mexico:
An Interpretative History *(Albuquerque: University of
New Mexico Press, 1977).*

CHAPTER ONE

Early Inhabitants

CLOVIS AND
FOLSOM PEOPLE

෨෬

Long before Europeans explored and settled New Mexico, human beings inhabited the area. They were, in fact, one of the main reasons for Spain to settle there. But these "pre–European contact" people had been in New Mexico (a name they never used) for at least some twelve thousand years. Early discoveries such as Clovis and Folsom hunters in eastern New Mexico speak to hunters and gatherers who lived in an environment much different from today's.

Scholars refer to this earliest of periods as the Pleistocene epoch. The last Ice Age was ending and as ice and cold climates receded north, a series of successive waves of people crossed the Bering Strait from Siberia to Alaska. The sea level was three hundred feet lower than it is today. As a result these early nomadic people were able to move from Asia to America overland. They probably traveled in small groups, hunting big game, now extinct, as they made their way southward along ice-free corridors. They took shelter wherever it could be found, using caves and rock shelters.

Some eleven thousand years ago a group of these early people hid in the tall grass and foliage that surrounded a marsh in what is now the Blackwater Draw near Clovis, New Mexico. They had found a place that drew game for its water. The marsh apparently was a magnet for the hunted as well as the hunters. The hunted included Colombian mammoths, cameloids, and horses.

Predators included large cats, wolves, and human beings. These last were on foot and they, unlike other predators, had learned to make stone tools and spear points from certain types of stone such as chert, commonly known as flint. But they, too, were hunted and lived precarious lives. A big cat, stone-edged weapons or not, must have struck terror into more than a few of these people.

So they waited for their potential prey to come to the marsh while fearing being stalked themselves. And when a large mammoth arrived, the group attacked with their spears. The attack would have required coordination among the hunters, who in the process performed acts of courage hard to imagine by today's standards. Once the animal was brought down and killed, the hunters waded into the water to butcher the exposed side of the beast, taking meat and maybe hide, leaving the submerged part intact. Many thousands of years later, in the 1930s, archaeologists discovered the evidence of this particular hunt as well as some others. After a long fight with mining operators and the government bureaucracy, a part of the site was preserved for study. The archaeologists learned about these early people and named them Clovis Man. Even though no human remains were found the bones of their kills, interspersed with distinctive fluted spear points, gave evidence to human existence at a defined time and place. Through radiocarbon dating the scholars were able to place the discoveries in Blackwater Draw as early as a little over eleven thousand years ago. This find was the earliest established for the Southwest and possibly represents the discovery of the earliest Americans.

Clovis Man became a standard as more Clovis sites (i.e., sites with Clovis points) were discovered across North America. Clovis existence has been pushed back to 12,000 years ago in North America. Interestingly enough a Clovis discovery was confirmed on the coast of Chile in South America that is 12,500 years old. This discovery is the oldest yet found and raises some questions. Did people arrive in South America a millennium before they moved into the Southwest? If so, how? Did they travel by water down the Pacific Coast? Or did they travel overland without leaving any evidence of the fact? Perhaps future discoveries will provide evidence predating the Chile site and will present a definitive explanation.

In the Southwest another hunter-gatherer people, which is called Folsom Man, came after the Clovis Man. Folsom Man dates from circa 8200 B.C., which is some two thousand years after the earliest Clovis culture. George McJunkin, a black cowboy and ex-slave who worked as a foreman on the Folsom Ranch in eastern New Mexico, first discovered evidence of this culture in 1908. He noticed some unusually large bones exposed in a gully after a rainstorm. He shared his discovery and eventually convinced some experts to visit the site. Subsequent investigations verified the value of McJunkin's keen observation. The Folsom information was important, for when the Clovis site was first excavated a few years later, the archaeologists were able to note that the older Clovis artifacts were under the Folsom artifacts, thus helping them understand that Clovis Man predated Folsom Man. In addition, they could see that Folsom Man had spear points distinct from those of Clovis Man. Folsom points found embedded among bison bones were much finer, smaller, and better crafted. And, perhaps because they are more recent, Folsom sites have yielded more and a larger variety of artifacts.

Over time people of the Southwest hunted less and gathered more. By the end of the Ice Age, around 3000 B.C., cultural differences had developed among groups, reflecting to some extent the slight environmental and topographical differences in which the peoples existed.

Then the climate began to change as the colder weather continued to recede north. The Clovis and subsequent Folsom people left with the climatic change and were replaced by a people characterized by various cultural traditions. These people are primarily called Archaic and, in the Southwest, have several names, the most common of which is Desert Dwellers.

The Archaic people of the Southwest are generally seen as the ancestors of the current Pueblo people inhabiting the Southwest. They are also seen as transitional people in that they, for the most part, moved from hunting and gathering to agriculture, which became the genesis for the Southwest's subsequent cultures.

The Archaic cultures of the Southwest shared commonalities such as rock art that is common for sites as widespread as around El Paso in west Texas, southeast Utah, and southern Texas. On the other hand, four distinct subgroups or traditions have been identified. These are the *San Dieguito* tradition in Arizona and California, who are the ancestors of the Colorado River peoples; the *Oshara* tradition in the north around the Four Corners area, who are the ancestors of the Anasazi, and the *Cochise* tradition in eastern Arizona and west-central New Mexico, who are the ancestors of the Mogollon and, probably, the Hohokam. The last tradition is an unnamed eastern subculture that existed in central and southern Texas. As the Archaic peoples progressed through this long period, which began as early as 6000 B.C. and ended around 500 B.C., they interacted with and affected each other.

Some experts split the period into two distinct parts. The first part dates from around 6000 B.C. to circa 2000 B.C. The Archaic people who lived during this period were hunters and gatherers who hunted and trapped smaller game like deer, antelope, and rodents. They fished and gathered seeds, nuts, and berries. Like their very lifestyles, the climate itself was in transition from wet to dry, cooler to warmer. They traveled in small groups, probably of extended families, and lived in makeshift dwellings made of branches. Some of these dwellings were set up on rises, from which game as well as potential enemies could be seen at a distance.

Around 4800 B.C. these people started digging wells as the water tables dropped and the climate became dryer. These wells were dug up to ten meters deep and hint of a people who were beginning to stay in place rather than roam. Between 3200 B.C. and 2000 B.C. the Archaic people began to construct small circular shadow pithouses. Sites usually have five to ten detached dwellings, which suggests that the Archaic people continued to operate in small groups. The second part of the Archaic period dates from circa 2000 B.C. to circa 500 B.C. By this time the Ice Age had ended. The climate was dry and the environment was varied, somewhat matching today's southwestern environment. The progression to agriculture accelerated as desert dwellers were forced to improvise to provide the water and foods necessary for survival. Hunter-gatherers work less to survive as they live in environments conducive to plentiful game, plant life, and water. As the climate became arid, however, the game and food became less plentiful, so people had to develop other more labor-intensive methods to sustain themselves. Knowledge of agriculture slowly entered the Southwest, basically from the south, and moved to the north, where it really took root among the Oshara people. The ancestral Hohokam and Mogollon, or Archaic Cochise tradition, were the first to learn to become gardeners, possibly as early as 2000 B.C. and at least by as late as 1000 B.C.

Whereas the Archaic people collected seeds as gatherers, the foodstuffs that would change the history of these people forever came from central Mexico. One was a type of grass that had been developed into corn. Squash was introduced into the Southwest at the same time as corn, between 1500 B.C. and 1000 B.C. Common beans arrived a few hundred years later. Not surprisingly, the *mano* and *metate*, grinding stones that were used to make flour from the seeds, came into use simultaneously with the introduction of these new crops. And, with flour, people stored as well as cooked food. By 1000 B.C. nomadic lifestyles were being replaced by a more settled way of life. But these people still did not qualify as complete sedentary types.

As mentioned earlier, agriculture caught on at a more rapid rate among the northern Oshara people. From 1500 B.C. to A.D. 200, when pottery first appeared in the Southwest, the spread of farming has led scholars to name this late Archaic period the "early agriculture period." Late Archaic period campsites dating to between 670 B.C. and 500 B.C. are strewn along the upper Rio Grande Valley, in the Pajarito Plateau in the Jémez Mountains, and along the volcanic escarpment known as La Bajada, which is southwest of Santa Fe. The descendents of these people still live in these areas.

So after almost six thousand years people had become seminomadic farmers and traders. They moved from migrating between temporary camps to creating semipermanent pithouses that may have been used seasonally. And, as agriculturists, these people became known as the Hohokam, Mogollon, and Anasazi cultures, which experts trace to most of the later southwestern Native American cultures.

*Mogollon cliff dwelling at Gila Cliffs by Silver City. Photograph by
O. C. Hinman. Courtesy Palace of the Governors (MNM/DCA 6205).*

CHAPTER TWO

A Large Sedentary World

THE HOHOKAM,
MOGOLLON, AND
ANASAZI PEOPLES

ᏏᎤᎧ

P ueblo Bonito, in Chaco Canyon in northwestern New Mexico, was
finished around 1130 A.D. and was a massive structure four stories
high containing seven hundred plastered rooms and thirty-three
kivas. The building was capable of housing up to twelve hundred people. All the Chacoan structures were made of stone. Details such as
"T"-shaped doorways demonstrate the masonry skills of the people.
And it is with good reason that their techniques are copied in modern
homes and institutions such as hotels.

Eventually the influence, if not the power, of the Chaco people
showed itself in the scores of outlier communities, one recently discovered as far away as southeastern New Mexico. Most of these communities had a Chacoan "great house," roadways, and a great kiva, among
other common features. The great houses had large-scale religious as

Aerial view of the ruins of Pueblo Bonito, 1931. Photo by
Big Sky Trails, Inc. (George Law). Photograph courtesy
Palace of the Governors (MNM/DCA 41797).

well as ceremonial dimensions and quite possibly served as seats for local lords overseeing trade and agriculture. The local farmers lived in humble dwellings, some gathered in smaller communities that were dominated by the outliers. And the trade extended to Mesoamerica.

The Chaco people are known for their roads. Much of what has been learned about the road system, if that is a proper description, has become the basis for many unanswered questions. These roads are highly engineered and straight. Rather than go around natural impediments they go over them. They are uniformly about thirty feet wide. Today, they are hard to see at ground level but from the air they are clearly delineated.

The two main Chaco roads radiate out to the north and south. The northern road connects to Aztec, while the southern road's destination, if any, has not been determined. The outlier communities, as well, have

Reconstruction of Pueblo Bonito in Chaco Canyon.
An oil painting by Robert M. Griffin, 1934. Photograph
courtesy Palace of the Governors (MNM/DCA 81171).

these roads but in every case so far studied the roads extend out for a mile or so and disappear. Some experts believe that these short roads to nowhere were used for ceremonial or religious purposes.

In the middle to late twelfth century the once flourishing Chaco Canyon people left their magnificent buildings to take up life elsewhere. Most scholars agree that the most immediate cause of this sudden demise was a long drought that began around 1090 A.D. As a lack of rainfall wrought havoc on the food supplies, people lost faith in their leadership. First the outliers were abandoned and then the canyon itself was deserted. Apparently there was a political move to save face by moving up the northern road to Aztec in the early 1100s. This attempt to reestablish power at Aztec did not last long, for within two generations this second area was abandoned. Some people believe that it was this group of Chaco people who left Aztec and tried to establish a new power base at Paquimé, far to the south in Casas Grandes, Chihuahua.

∞

Some Chaco people moved south into various areas where the Mogollon people had settled and were still living in relatively small communities made up of random pithouses located by their planted fields. One branch of the Mogollon, called the Mimbres, lived in the mountainous area of Silver City in western New Mexico. Heavily influenced by the Anasazi in architecture as well as pottery, for which the Mimbres are famous, these people, too, were ancestral Puebloans. Other branches such as the Jornado Mogollon learned to survive in the desert country in Arizona and southern New Mexico.

The influx from the north had a profound influence on the Mogollon, who soon abandoned their pithouses to construct Anasazi-style rock pueblos. Like the Anasazi, the Mogollon (with their Chacoan brethren) created cliff dwellings, the most famous of which can be seen at the Gila Cliff Dwellings National Monument near Silver City. The dwellings were built in the last third of the thirteenth century and were occupied for no more than thirty years.

The Mogollon territory ranged from the Sacramento Mountains east of Alamogordo to western Arizona, and south to below Casas Grandes. One of the great Pueblo ruins existing today can be seen at Paquimé. Recent study has pointed out an interesting observation that from Mesa Verde and Chaco Canyon in the north, down through the Gila Cliff Dwellings to Paquimé in the south, a direct north-south axis is formed. There is no doubt that exchange took place and the various cultures influenced one another. From corn, squash, and beans moving north to architectural techniques moving south, the ancestral Puebloan world was expansive.

∞

Farther west and south on the even more unforgiving lands in Arizona and northern Mexico, the Hohokam learned to cope with their hot and dry environment. More than three thousand years ago they began to adopt a more settled agricultural life and their population increased as they established villages and developed irrigation systems and pottery. Water, of course, was the key and the Hohokam built a vast network of irrigation canals, some of which were fifty feet wide and carried enough water to sustain as many as fifty or sixty thousand people. Their villages were established at regular intervals along the canals. Ditches ran off the main canals to water crops of corn, beans, squash, cotton, and agave over thousands of acres. They apparently produced enough foodstuffs to export while they imported shells from the west coast. They developed a complex social and economic system.

While the majority of people lived in small dwellings built of mud, sticks, and branches, the Hohokam did have large-scale public structures, the most obvious of which were the large platform mounds and their ballcourts, some two hundred of which have been found in Arizona. The Hohokam began building the mounds after 1100 A.D. Some of the tops of these mounds were larger than a football field. At first, the mounds were used as ritual sites and were topped with small temples. The community lived in clustered houses surrounded by mud walls around the bases of these mounds. Around 1300 A.D., people began to move their dwellings to the tops of the mounds, thus indicating the appearance of a stratified society.

The Hohokam were an amazing society not only for their construction, but because they survived in a harsh, challenging environment for centuries. However, by the time that the first Spanish explorations passed through the Hohokam territory the canals, mounds, ballcourts, and towns had been abandoned. Archaeological evidence indicates that the end came around 1450 A.D. While not definitive, theory suggests that the Hohokam dispersed. Some became today's Pima and Tohono O'Odham (Papago) people still living in the same area. Others moved north and west to join the ancestral Puebloan peoples, most notably at the Hopi pueblos. Most likely, too, some Hohokam became a part of the multiethnic society that flourished at Casas Grandes around Paquimé.

∞

In the north Aztec remained abandoned for a few years and then was reoccupied by Chacoans who had first moved to Mesa Verde. These people and their descendants would stay in the Aztec and San Juan river basin from about 1110 A.D. until 1275. The area's population grew rapidly.

Within one two-mile stretch, at least, thirteen great kivas, many earthworks, quarries, and three separate road systems were engineered and constructed. This all happened as Chaco Canyon was being abandoned, an exile that became complete by 1140 A.D. Aztec, in effect, became the new Chaco.

One interesting discovery at Aztec was an unusual burial. The individual was important, for he was wrapped in a turkey feather blanket and buried with jewelry, bowls, jars, what may have been wooden swords, and a basketry shield. What was different is this person's height, for he was six feet, two inches tall! He was a giant in his day.

Another pueblo near the San Juan River yielded an important historical detail—a tragic fire. The pueblo, now called Salmon Ruins, once had been a three-hundred-room structure that, like Aztec, was abandoned in the last quarter of the thirteenth century. Salmon was a Chaco site built in the classic great-house design and then deserted after two generations. Unlike Aztec, Salmon was not quickly reoccupied. Rather, the pueblo remained vacant for almost a century before anyone moved back.

The new inhabitants of Salmon were Chacoans from Mesa Verde. They renovated the place, adding kivas and expanding the size to its ultimate three hundred rooms.

Around 1260 the pueblo suffered a catastrophic fire. Like many fires it started in one place, grew out of control, and spread. Some fifty children were initially evacuated from the point of danger. Apparently for safety's sake, the children were gathered on a great kiva roof and here tragedy struck. Weakened by the heat of the fire, the roof collapsed, all the children falling into the kiva, where the temperatures were so hot that the sand on the floor was fused into glass. Today, we can only imagine the grief and sorrow of that moment. Within two decades after this horrific event, Salmon was again abandoned.

∞

As noted above, the Chaco people also eventually inhabited Mesa Verde. Rather than move into an area and start anew, the Chacoans inhabited an area already settled by Anasazi who had lived in pithouses there as early as 600 A.D. and moved into surface dwellings around 750 A.D. (the Pueblo I period). As was the natural process, the clusters of rooms slowly developed into pueblos, some containing dwellings with as many as one hundred contiguous rooms and housing as many as six hundred people. These pueblos first developed on mesa tops with irrigated farming on the river bottom. From 900 A.D. to 1100 (the Pueblo II period), a population decline took place.

Around 1200 A.D., almost a century after the apex of Chaco Canyon's development, the Mesa Verde people built and moved into the cliff dwellings for which they have become famous. These new spectacular villages were somewhat isolated from one another. Even today they seem unreal, and photographic images do not do them justice. Most of the people maintained mesatop villages located above the cliff dwellings. Unlike the other Anasazi from Chaco Canyon, these people apparently did not carve out a road system, which is excusable given the rough terrain in which they lived.

The people from the villages did communicate. They met along the trails to sources of water, while hunting and gathering, as well as at shared village ceremonies held at what appear to have been common ceremonial centers at places like "Sun Temple" and "Fire Temple." The surviving ruins of some of these villages are a source of wonder to visitors, for they were constructed with great precision in seemingly impossible places. The villages now have names like Spruce Tree House, Cliff Palace, Balcony House, Long House, and Mug House, among others. They are evidence of a vibrant society, yet, as has been noted in the histories of other Anasazi sites, people seemed to pass through Mesa Verde. The area seems to have had at once an influx of people from the abandonment of Chaco Canyon and a migration out to settle new areas like Aztec and Salmon. With this changing demography the great cliff dwellings of Mesa Verde lasted only one century. A final note of interest is that the Montezuma Valley near Cortez, Colorado, was settled at the same time and had a much larger population.

By 1300 A.D. all the great Anasazi sites in the Four Corners area had been abandoned. The drought at the end of the eleventh century that eventually caused the downfall of Chaco Canyon was followed by the drought of 1276, which lasted twenty-three years. It is no coincidence that the two droughts are perfectly timed with the respective abandonments of Chaco and then the whole area. Neither is it a coincidence that the creation stories of these people's descendants tell of a people moving and searching for the right place to settle and make their home.

Thus, in the 1300s, people took their possessions, their knowledge, and cultures and searched for a new, more hospitable place to live. By now migration had become a part of their tradition. The majority of these people moved into the Rio Grande river valley or its tributaries, such as the Chama River basin, where some Anasazi had preceded them. Moving to the Chama basin was a natural and relatively short move across the continental divide from the Four Corners region. Others moved to the areas of Zuni and Acoma, a known territory of abandoned Chaco outliers. Indeed, maybe the origins of Zuni and Acoma are as Chaco outliers. It is important to note here that the ancient cultures so far described have survived into the present. They never ceased to exist but continued to do what they always did. They moved and evolved. And, interestingly enough, the various pueblos kept in contact with one another through trade, warfare, and common language groups.

∞

This new period is called the Rio Grande Classic Period. It begins with a migration in about 1300. The Pajarito Plateau, in the Jémez Mountains beside the Rio Grande, had been sparsely settled since as early as 600 A.D. The first large colonization did not occur until about the late twelfth century, a time between the two droughts and after Chaco Canyon's end in 1140. The ultimate decline of the entire Four Corners area, including the Colorado Plateau, resulted in a second large influx of people. The population of the Pajarito Plateau as well as the northern Rio Grande Valley grew dramatically. Several new pueblos developed, such as Puye, now on the Santa Clara Reservation, and at Bandelier National Monument, built into the cliffs using the naturally formed cavities in the volcanic tuff. The builders were able to use harder stone tools, hammers, and chisels to hollow out and expand the cavities into rooms. They then added masonry houses in front.

They also built on the valley floors as well as on small rises above their water source. Some of these new villages were laid out and centered on plazas, which became more common. Others, however, stretched along streets, possibly to take advantage of passive solar heat. All had kivas of various sizes and shapes.

The people also developed pottery that differed from that of their ancestors. They experimented and developed new shapes and a new black-on-red color scheme. There was a trend back to large population centers, possibly for defensive reasons, which resulted in the development of a more centralized sociopolitical order. But the Pueblo people also continued many previous traditions. Aside from their structures and building techniques, the most obvious of these was the creation and then abandonment of dwellings. Although not as drastic as previous abandonments, this pattern continued. For example, within two hundred years after moving onto the Pajarito Plateau, all the people had abandoned their homes to move into villages along the Rio Grande. By 1500 the Pueblo people had developed villages and language groups that are identifiable today.

Movement east, across the Rio Grande and beyond, was the longest trek. Nevertheless, some small family groups did it. Mogollon as well as Anasazi groups drifted into the southeastern and northeastern parts of New Mexico between 700 and 900 A.D. By 1300 these people had either joined other groups along the Rio Grande or concentrated in some of the more favorable areas east of the mountains. One of these pueblos, Pecos, or Cicuye, as the Spanish first named it, became the largest pueblo in New Mexico by the middle of the sixteenth century. Other pueblos, such as Quarai, Abó, Gran Quivira, San Marcos, Galisteo, and San Cristóbal, joined Pecos and Taos to the north to become trade and contact centers with the nomadic Indians coming off the plains. These pueblos not only grew in size, but they also became relatively wealthy. They also served as a buffer or first line of defense for their sedentary cousins to the west against the nomadic people from the plains.

All these newly developed pueblos had water-capturing systems with some kind of irrigation. Many had become adept at dry farming. Villages by permanent streams and rivers were less dependent on rainfall. Still, all were vulnerable to drought. As had happened earlier in their history, a drought struck in the late 1500s. As a result the Pajarito Plateau was abandoned as well as a great many of the villages in the Chama River basin. The eastern pueblos coalesced. With a few exceptions all the pueblos that survive today date to this period.

Ancient Observations

Interest in the sky and the study of celestial bodies has been long-standing in New Mexico. From the Very Large Array to the Sacramento Peak Observatory set up to study the sun, to the state's many research laboratories, New Mexico clearly has been involved in the science of astronomy and the study of outer space. Yet this interest is not new; as shown by the Zia sun symbol that was taken from a Pueblo pot and selected for the state flag in the 1920s, this interest in the sky dates back to ancient times.

The relatively new field of archaeoastronomy has firmly established that the ancestors of the Pueblo Indians looked at the sky in a deliberate and methodical manner. They studied and plotted the movement of the sun, the moon, and other stellar objects. The inhabitants of Chaco Canyon may have recorded in a petroglyph (a drawing or carving on rock) an observed supernova or star explosion in 1054 A.D.!

Agricultural people throughout history and around the world have been concerned with calendrical observations. Religious as well as secular activities are based on these seasonal observations. This is evident among the modern Pueblo peoples, both from current observation and from late nineteenth-, early twentieth-century studies by such noted scholars as Frank Cushing and Matilda Coxe Stevenson. They noted, for example, the Zuni method for sun observation—tracing sunrises and sunsets at different locations on the horizon from day to day as the sun moves from one solstice to the other. Another example is the roof of the Bear Clan house on the First Mesa of the Hopi pueblos, which is used to note horizon locations of the sun at sunset.

The symbols used for these observations can be connected to symbols used in dozens of sites in the Four Corners region. And this has opened up a whole new field of study, for now such symbols and their locations must be seen in a different context. Researchers have been able to document many sites where sun symbols or symbols with concentric circles have been located intentionally at an observation point from which the "sun priest" or assigned person can watch the sun or other celestial bodies in relation to well-defined landmarks. These observation stations have proven to be especially accurate for calendrical purposes. The station found at Wijiji in Chaco Canyon is a great example, for it

Solstice window at Pueblo Bonito. Photograph by W. James Judge. Courtesy National Park Service, Chaco Center HHP, slide no. 821.

lines up with an obvious large natural rock pillar on a well-defined horizon. As observed from the station, the sun rises directly behind the rock pillar in spectacular fashion at winter solstice.

The Anasazi as well as the Hohokam peoples advanced beyond using natural phenomena for their celestial studies. They used alignments of architectural features in combination with drawings and the horizon for recording their astronomical observations. These alignments ranged from small rock huts to an ingenious "instrument" of rock and shadow at Fajada Butte to actual construction of buildings.

Pueblo Bonito still has two third-story, exterior corner windows that may have been used to record sunrise at the winter solstice. The great kiva at Casa Rinconada has interior markings related to solstices and equinoxes. And Casa Grande in Arizona, a rectangular three-story building constructed around 1300 A.D., has a number of slots and portholes that seem to have a calendrical purpose. One slot on the top floor definitely aligns with the summer solstice sunset. Could this building, orientated to the cardinal directions, be, in part, an early observatory? And were there more?

Surely, these early ancestors to many of today's New Mexicans developed a good knowledge of the sky. From that knowledge they based the timing of their ceremonials and planting of their crops. This knowledge continues to be a basis of cultural life cycles. The Zia sun symbol is truly appropriate to New Mexico's history and cultural heritage.

In addition to natural problems, the Pueblo people suffered two shocks to their world within a hundred-year period. The first occurred with the arrival of the Athabascan or Apache and Navajo people, as late as 1500, and the second, by far a larger shock, was the arrival of Spanish Europeans and their Indian allies from central Mexico in the 1530s and 1540s.

Sometime near 1500 there was a period when people living in smaller villages started moving and creating new towns, joining relatives in other towns. While this is partly attributed to drought, as already mentioned, this increased activity is also a reaction to the latest and largest influx of Athabascan nomadic people. These hunter-gatherers are not related to the Pueblo people or their ancestors. Nor were they related to earlier hunter-gatherers in the area such as, for example, the Ute Indians, who are related to the Comanche Indians and descendant from hunter-gatherers in the Southwest.

The Athabascan people in the Southwest are related to Native Americans in Alaska, Canada, and along the Pacific Coast. They migrated into New Mexico from northwest Canada starting about 1200 A.D. Like nomadic people throughout history they raided sedentary people to augment their food supply. Sedentary people were convenient and natural targets for nomads, especially at harvest time. Both the Pueblos and subsequently the Spanish villages would suffer from nomadic raids. Some experts argue that the early arrival of the Navajos may have helped cause the disruption of the Anasazi in Chaco Canyon. All agree that they did disrupt the Pueblos around 1500.

The Athabascans, who come down through history as the Navajos, Mescaleros, Jicarillas, and Chiricahuas, among others, all settled in the Southwest, including New Mexico. They were a splintered or decentralized people. They lived in groups that constantly moved, residing in temporary dwellings. They did not see themselves as one people. Each of the Athabascan groups developed differently in their customs and religion.

The Navajos or Diné were the largest of the Athabaskan groups and probably the most troublesome to the Pueblos. As a result of their more constant contacts with the Pueblos, they became more settled than the other Athabaskan groups. They first moved into the Southwest to an area they called Dinetah, occupying the area surrounding the Largo and

Gobernador Canyons. The Navajo Nation regards this northwestern place in New Mexico as its original homeland.

Aside from warfare, the Navajos also traded with the Pueblos. They began to build seasonal homes called hogans and to farm, especially corn, both of which they learned from the Pueblos. The term "Navajo" may come from a Tewa Pueblo word meaning "arroyo of cultivated fields." They developed an intricate religion that they were able to communicate through sandpaintings. Importantly, they traveled great distances to trade and raid.

The Pueblos, perhaps reflecting their antecedents from Mogollon and Anasazi cultures, developed into separate but similar cultures. They had four language groups, three of which are in New Mexico. Today, Azteco-Zuni is spoken at the Zuni pueblos and Keresan is the language of Santo Domingo, Cochiti, Santa Ana, San Felipe, Zia, Acoma, and Laguna pueblos. The Tanoan language is broken into three subgroups. The people at the pueblos of Taos, Picurís, Sandia, and Isleta speak Tiwa, whereas Tewa is spoken at the pueblos of Santa Clara, San Ildefonso, San Juan, Pojoaque, Tesuque, and Nambé, and Towa is the language at Jémez Pueblo and was the language of Pecos Pueblo.

When the Europeans arrived, the area ranging from Socorro in the south to Taos in the north and extending west to the Hopi villages numbered some seventy-five to eighty towns. Most of these towns had between two hundred and three hundred inhabitants with the overall population estimated to be between thirty and eighty thousand people. Scholars still debate the figures and most agree that the Spanish high-end estimate is exaggerated.

The towns were made up of multistoried buildings with no doors or windows on the first or bottom floors, which were used for storage. Most of the structures took advantage of the sun for warmth in the winter. The western pueblos were constructed of sandstone. Those in the Rio Grande basin were made of puddled mud while stone was the material of choice for the eastern pueblos.

The Pueblo people had long established themselves as sedentary farmers who had learned to rotate crops. They supplemented what they grew and collected with trade. They had developed a structured, sophisticated society with clans made up of blood relatives and moieties organized around seasons, events, or survival strategies such as

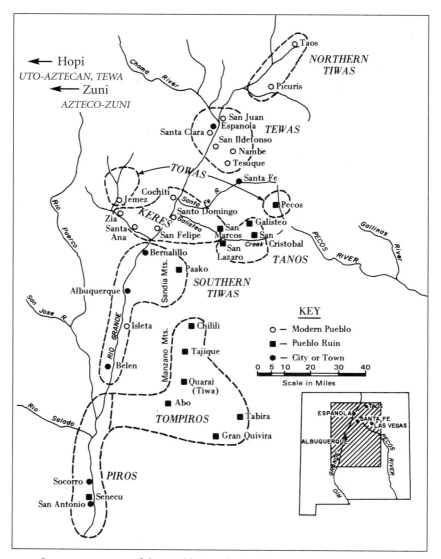

Language groups of the Pueblo People. In Myra Ellen Jenkins and Albert H. Schroeder, A Brief History of New Mexico *(Albuquerque: University of New Mexico Press, 1974).*

defense. Religion was a major part of life. They worshiped many gods, and believed in creation and emergence from the Sipapu, that place where their ancestors entered this world from an underground spiritual world. They made Kachinas or other figures that represent the spirits of ancestors. All of this exists today as the descendants of the Mogollon, Hohokam, and Anasazi continue to adapt and thrive.

regni ch'io dico, all'hora fi potria meglio vedere fenza metter à pericolo la mia perfona, & D
laffar per quefto di dar relation delle cofe vedute. folamente viddi dalla bocca della campagna fette villaggi ragioneuoli,alquāto lontani, in vna valle di fotto molto frefca & di molto
buona terra,donde vfciuano molti fiumi,hebbi informatiōe che in ḡlla era molto oro,et che
gli habitatori l'adoperano in vafi & palettine, con lequali fi radono & leuano via il fudore,&
che fono gente che non confentono che quelli d'altra parte della campagna contrattino con
loro,& non mi feppero dir la caufa. Qui pofi due croci,& tolfi il poffeffo di tutta la campagna & valle per la maniera & ordine delli poffeffi tolti da me di fopra conforme alla inftrut-
tione, & di li profegui il ritorno del mio viaggio con la maggior preffa ch'io potei fin ch'io
arriuai alla terra di fan Michiele della prouincia di Culiacan,credendo trouar in quel luogo
Francefco Vazquez di Coronado Gouernator della nuoua Galitia,& non trouandolo pro
fegui il mio cammino fino alla città di Compoftella doue lo trouai. Non fcriuo qui molte altre particolarità,perche non fono pertinenti à quefto cafo. folamente dico quello ch'io viddi,& mi fu detto delle terre per doue andai,& di quelle che hebbi informatione.

RELATIONE   CHE   MANDO'   FRANCESCO

Vazquez di Coronado, Capitano Generale della gente che fu mandata
in nome di Sua Maefta al paefe nouamente fcoperto , quel che
fucceffe nel viaggio dalli ventidua d' Aprile di quefto anno   E
M D X L. che parti da Culiacan per innanzi,& di quel che
trouò nel paefe doue andaua.

Francefco Vazquez con effercito parte di Culiacan,et doppo il patire diuerfi incommodi nel mal viag
gio,gionge alla Valle de i Caraconi, la ritroua fterile di Maiz:per hauerne,manda nella valle
detta del Signore,ha relatione della grandezza della valle di Caraconi, & di
quelli popoli, & di alcune Ifole pofte in quelle coftiere.

Lli ventiduoi del Mefe d'Aprile paffato,parti dalla prouincia di Culiacan
con parte dell'effercito & con l'ordine che io fcriffi à V.S.& fecondo il fuc-
ceffo tengo per certo che fi in douinò à non metter tutto l'effercito vnito in
quefta imprefa,perche fono ftati cofi grandi i trauagli & mancamento della
vettouaglia che credo che in tutto quefto anno non fi poteffe effettuar la
imprefa,et gia che fi effettuaffe farebbe con gran perdita di gente,perche co
me fcriffi à V.S. io feci il viaggio di Culiacan in ottanta giorni di ftrada la-
quale,io & quei gentil'huomini à cauallo miei compagni portāmo fu le fpalle & ne noftri ca
ualli,vn poco di vettouaglia, in modo che da quefta impoi nō portammo niun di noi d altre   F
robbe neceffarie tanto che paffaffe vna libra, & con tutto cio, & con l'efferfi meffa in quefta
poca vettouaglia che portammo tutta quella regola & ordine pofsibile, ci mancò , & non è
da farfene marauiglia,perche il câmino è afpro & lungo,& fra gli archibufi che li portauano
nel fallir delle montagne & cofte,& nel paffar de i fiumi ci fi guafto la maggior parte del
Maiz:& perche io mando à V.S.dipinto quefto viaggio nō le diro in cio altro per ḡfta mia.
Trenta leghe prima che fi arriuaffe al luogo che il padre Prouinciale nella fua relatione
cofi ben diceua,mandai Melchior Diaz con quindici da cauallo innanzi , ordinandogli che
faceffe di due giornate vna , accioche haueffi efaminato il tutto quando io giongeffi :ilqua-
le,camminò quattro giorni per certe montagne afprifsime,et non trouò quiui ne da viuere,
ne gēte,ne information di alcuna cofa, eccetto che trouò due ò tre pouere villette, di venti
ò trenta capanne l'una,& da gli habitatori di effa feppe che da li auanti non fi trouaua fe non
afprifsime montagne che continouauano,difabitate da tutte le genti, & perche era cofa per-
duta non volfi di qui mandar di cio meffo à V.S. diedi difpiacere à tutti i compagni,che vna
cofa tanto lodata , & di che il padre haueua detto tante cofe fi foffe trouato tanto al contra
rio,& fi fece giudicio che il rimanente foffe tutto di quella forte.Et veduto io quefto procu
rai di rallegrargli al meglio che io potei,dicendogli che V.S. fempre hebbe oppinione che
quefto viaggio foffe vna cofa gittata via,& che doueìsimo metter il noftro pēfiero in quelle
fette

Chapter heading for the first published account of Francisco
Vásquez de Coronado's 1540–1541 expedition into New Mexico.
From Giovanni Batista Ramusio, Navigationi et Viaggi . . . *(1556).*
Original in the Fray Angélico Chávez Library. Photograph courtesy
Palace of the Governors (MNM/DCA 152669).

CHAPTER THREE

New World/New People

EARLY EUROPEAN
EXPLORATION

ᘓᘐ

After thousands of years of living and evolving in this desperate land, a completely new, unrelated, and unknown people moved into the Southwest and gave it a name in the language of the Zuni's. *Cíbola*, or "land of the buffalo," was the first name, which would soon be replaced by *La Nueva México*, "Another Mexico," before finally becoming *New Mexico*.

These new people were Europeans from the recently unified country of Spain. They were an adventurous sort whose long history had conspired to make them world explorers. Their country, along with Portugal, formed the Iberian Peninsula, which was a geographic formation with water on four sides and that jutted toward Africa. The peninsula was, at once, connected to and separated from the rest of Europe by the Pyrenees Mountains.

The Iberian Peninsula was originally occupied by natives (called Iberos), Basques (origin unknown), Phoenicians (1000 B.C.), Greeks (650 B.C.), Celts in the north (600 B.C.), Romans (218 B.C.), Visigoths (476 A.D.), and Muslims out of Africa (711 A.D.). Aside from the almost seven-hundred-year occupation by Rome that left language, law, and architecture, the most defining moment in the history of the people who came to New Mexico was the almost eight centuries' occupation of Spain by the Moors and its reconquest by the Christians. Pushed far into the northern mountains, Christians began a crusade to retake their peninsula from the Muslim people who took it from them. In the course of this long drawn-out religious conflict, St. James the Apostle, under the name of Santiago Matamoros or St. James the Moor Killer, became the patron of the Christian forces. El Cid, a real person who fought against and with Moors, would become a legendary symbol of St. James. Fighting on behalf of Catholicism became a sacred mission. The pope declared the reconquest of Iberia the first official crusade of the Catholic Church in reaction to the first recorded *jihad* proclaimed by Al Mansar, a hunchbacked and sadistic caliph based in Córdoba. The reconquest, which took almost eight hundred years, defined the Spanish character.

A number of historical events occurred in Europe around the end of the fifteenth century, just as the Pueblo people were coalescing in and around the Rio Grande Valley and reacting to an influx of Athabaskan people. On the peninsula, the marriage of Isabel of Castile and Ferdinand of Aragón created the nation of Spain. They, in turn, concentrated on solidifying Spain by waging war, first on opposing political factions and second on the Moors, whom they defeated at Granada and subsequently expelled from Spain. Caught up in the religious fervor that had been the fuel for the reconquest, the Catholic kings, as Ferdinand and Isabel were called, used their offices and those of the Inquisition to assure that their new nation would be Catholic. Partially as a result of the victory at Granada in 1492, Isabel granted permission to Christopher Columbus to sail west in quest of a shorter, more direct route to Asia. His success would ultimately triumph over Portugal's more fruitful attempts to get to the same place by sailing south and then east around Africa.

Fortunately for Columbus (who was called Colón in Spanish), a heretofore unknown continent that would be called America, after an

Italian mapmaker, interfered with his westward voyage. Had America not been there Columbus and his men most likely would have perished at sea, for they seriously underestimated the earth's circumference and projected Asia to be located about where they first sighted land, in what is today known as the Caribbean Sea.

This was a new world for the Europeans. They in turn represented a new world for the Native Americans. The Indians, as Columbus mistakenly identified these people, and their land became a natural and new theater for the European veterans of religious wars. Imagine the new sense of curiosity and adventure, if not wonder, that Columbus's voyages created. And the incentive of reward, both personal and celestial, cannot be overlooked.

Within decades, Spanish explorers, followed by settlers, spread throughout America.* Hernán Cortés and Francisco Pizarro, both from the poor, landlocked region of Spain called Extremadura, led conquests of the Aztecs in Mexico by 1522 and the Incas in Perú by 1532–34. Francisco de Orellana, also from Extremadura, floated down the length of the Amazon River. Magellan, a Portuguese sailing for Spain, led a crew that was the first to circumnavigate the world. From 1535 to 1553, the Spanish under Diego de Almagro and Pedro de Valdivia had explored and settled southern South America, where they met continued resistance from the Araucanian Indians. Valdivia's exploits were memorialized in a book-length epic poem written by one of his officers, named Alonso de Ercilla y Zuniga. Today, that poem, titled *La Araucana*, is required reading throughout Hispanic America. Ercilla's poem, published in Spain, would be mentioned by Antonio Cervantes as one of the works to be saved in Don Quixote's library and became the basis, if not inspiration, of a second epic poem, which would become a part of New Mexico's literary history, Gaspar de Villagrá's *La Historia de la Nueva Mexico*.

The Spanish became interested in the land of the Pueblo Indians in the far north when Pánfilo de Narváez, who failed to capture and arrest Cortés, losing an eye in the process, was sent on a failed expedition to Florida. Four men survived the expedition and were washed ashore near present-day Galveston, Texas, in 1528. From there, the local Indians

---

In the Spanish-speaking world North and South America are seen as one continent. "America" or "the Americas" refers to all the lands of what the English-speaking world considers two continents.

The Sopaipilla

For years, New Mexicans have bragged about their food—their chile, their blue corn tortillas, posole, and their unleavened bread, called the *sopaipilla*. The sopaipilla has always seemed to be something unique to New Mexico and, therefore, mentioned with local pride. Sopaipillas could not be found in other parts of the Southwest or even Mexico, where a request for a sopaipilla merely elicits quizzical stares.

The New Mexican sopaipilla is a light bread made of wheat flour and fried. It looks like a small pillow, for it is hollow inside. It is delivered warm to the table and is not more than five or six inches square. New Mexicans pinch off a corner and pour honey inside. The honey, combined with the bread, takes the bite, that is to say the hotness, out of chile. So, aside from its good taste, it has a special gastronomical function. In other parts of the world, honey is replaced with powdered sugar that is sprinkled on the outside of the bread.

The sopaipilla is a part of New Mexico's history, but it is not unique to New Mexico. This type of bread is found in different parts of the Hispanic world and is usually called *buñuelo*, *torta frita*, or fry bread. The English name hints that here is an example of a Spanish contribution to the Native American world, for Navajo fry bread is a larger sopaipilla and the wheat used to make it is also a Spanish introduction to the Americas.

New Mexicans distinguish the sopaipilla from the buñuelo by shape. In New Mexico the buñuelo is usually round with a hole or indentation in the middle, while in Argentina, for example, the sopaipilla is shaped like the New Mexican buñuelo.

"Sopaipilla" as a name or word is not known in Spain today, and it possibly reflects the antiquated, colonial Spanish language that survives

enslaved them, after which they escaped and began an odyssey during which they would travel on foot westward. They survived by befriending the various Natives whom they encountered. They claimed to be gods and as they progressed they apparently gained fame. Finally, in 1536, Álvar Núñez Cabeza de Vaca, Alonso de Castillo Maldonado, Andrés Dorantes, and his Moorish slave, Estevan, were captured by illegal Spanish slave traders near Culiacán, Mexico. They had traveled in some New Mexican Spanish. Research into the history of the language reveals that the word had its origin in Arabic, as does a third of the current Spanish language. The name came from the Arabic "súppa," which originally described bread after it had been dipped or dunked in a sauce or gravy. Over the years the term became Hispanicized to "sopaipa," and finally became the diminutive "sopaipilla" that came to the Americas. This legacy of the Moorish occupation of the Iberian Peninsula is also a part of New Mexico's heritage. The vast majority of people who left Spain for the Americas originated from the southwestern provinces of Spain, where the Moorish occupation had its strongest influence. Moreover, they traveled through the southern province of Andalusia. So, a regional term with Arabic origins traveled to the distant "kingdom" of New Mexico to be preserved through the years. Meanwhile, in Spain the name faded from memory.

In parts of South America, especially the regions of San Juan and Mendoza in western Argentina and into neighboring Chile, people make the same bread and call it a sopaipilla. Perhaps not surprisingly, these South American regions have a lot of similarities with New Mexico. They are located at the base of the mountains, are arid, landlocked, and relatively poor. They share a Spanish colonial history dating from the sixteenth century, and many of the Spanish who migrated to them came from, and through, Andalusia. They migrated with the sopaipilla as a food at a time when its original name was still used.

So, two distant regions of what was once a part of the Spanish empire have many things in common. None of the commonalities are more interesting than the sopaipilla and both regions can lay claim to their special bread with pride.

from the Gulf Coast across Texas and northern Mexico and down the West Coast. After eight years in the north, far away from their own people, it is no wonder that they were taken for Indians. It is also no wonder that Cabeza de Vaca, who would write of his adventure, came to appreciate the people and their respective cultures that he encountered.

News of their "rescue" spread. The viceroy, Antonio de Mendoza, quickly summoned them for an audience. They shared the knowledge and information that they had learned among the Indians in the north. Of particular interest was the tidbit that somewhere even farther to the north a rich civilization of people lived in towns or cities.

This information attracted the interest of the viceroy, who had them present the same information to his advisors. The idea of a rich civilization in the far north appealed to the minds of a people who had left their homes in Europe, crossed an ocean, and discovered civilizations in Mexico and Perú that were beyond anything that they had imagined. And they had large imaginations, for, while Cervantes would poke fun at such romanticism, the period was rife with possibilities. There were the lost tribes of Israel, the lost continent of Atlantis, the giant women of Amazonia, and the Seven Bishops who fled the Iberian Peninsula with the Moorish occupation. This last myth became confused with the myth of the Seven Cities of Cíbola, which would soon surface in connection with New Mexico. And all these tales and more had been published in popular books of knights-errant and adventure.

Suffice to say that the Spanish in the Americas were in some ways living out their imaginations. They had found great civilizations with cities as large as any in Europe, wealth beyond belief, and exotic customs. All this had been encountered in Central and South America. Tales of cities to the north made sense. Anything was possible.

Here was another chance for fame and wealth. Here, too, was a chance for the Crown to continue its crusade and fulfill its obligation to the church. With the 1494 Treaty of Tordesillas, Pope Urban VI divided the world in half between Spain and Portugal. Spain could explore and claim everything to the west of one hundred leagues west of the Azores and Cape Verde Islands. Portugal had all the lands east. The only obligation for both countries was that they had a moral responsibility to convert all the non-Christians that they encountered in their new lands. This was an obligation that the Spanish Crown took seriously. This became especially so in light of another event that took place around 1500. In 1517, Martin Luther, in an attempt to reform the church, began a movement that gave birth to Protestantism. England, under Elizabeth I, would take the lead in what came to be called the Reformation. Spain, under Carlos I (also known as Carlos V the Holy Roman Emperor) and his son Felipe II took up the defense of the church and led the Counter-Reformation. Following suit, the

Spanish Inquisition turned its attention to finding and punishing heretical Lutherans. This European schism would have its effect on the Americas, including New Mexico.

The viceroy in Mexico, then called New Spain, decided to be cautious with these new tales from the north, so he organized a scouting expedition. None of the Spanish survivors from the north wanted to return to the wilderness. However, the slave, Estevan, had no choice and perhaps even looked forward to returning to a place where he enjoyed more freedom. In 1539, Viceroy Mendoza sent Estevan with a Franciscan friar, Marcos de Niza, north to confirm the stories. The priest had been in Perú with Pizarro and was used to hardship and travel.

The two men headed north with Indian carriers, initially following in reverse the route Estevan had traveled earlier. They moved up the western side of Mexico. At some point, Estevan went ahead of the Franciscan. He used the Indian carriers to send messages back to his partner, who was following at a slower pace. The arrangement, so the story is told, was for Estevan to send crosses back, the size of which would indicate the importance of the message. Eventually the messengers were returning with crosses as large as they were.

Here the story of this scouting expedition gets hazy. Estevan, who presumably reverted to using the technique that had resulted in his survival in his earlier trek, started claiming that he represented God. The technique worked as he continued north into present-day Arizona, through the ancient lands of the Hohokam, and then east into New Mexico, the lands of the Mogollon and Anasazi. He came upon the first of the Pueblo villages at Zuni.

The Pueblos, as previously noted, had developed religions with long-established traditions. How did this new person fit in? What was he? Apparently, the Zunis tested Estevan's alleged divinity, for he was tossed off a mesa's edge and killed.

The Mexican Indians accompanying Estevan witnessed his death and rushed to warn Fray Marcos. Again, the story is unclear, for Marcos de Niza returned to Mexico City to tell of having seen cities of gold, which became the "Seven Cities of Cíbola."

The Franciscan allegedly claimed to have continued his trip north in spite of the news of Estevan's death. He traveled to see one or more of the Zuni pueblos from a distance, presumably to avoid being put to the same test as Estevan. Indeed, there might have been as many as seven Indian villages at Zuni. How they became known as golden is one of history's unanswered questions.

The viceroy did not hesitate to share the priest's tale. Now was the time to form a true expedition to go to this distant and newly visited land. He, personally, would invest his own funds to help pay for the venture. In Francisco Vásquez de Coronado, a minor noble and friend, the viceroy found a man who could cover the rest of the expenses as well as lead the expedition.

Vásquez de Coronado, who was the governor of Nueva Galicia, was a Castilian-born Spaniard who had attended the University of Salamanca. He would lead an expedition of over thirteen hundred people and the necessary amount of livestock to feed them. With all their supplies, some three hundred Spanish *conquistadores*, many mounted and in armor, plus a thousand Mexican Indian carriers and servants, gathered in formation at the town of Compostela in Nueva Galicia, where, before Viceroy Antonio de Mendoza, they swore allegiance to God and the king. The spectacle of this grand army with the officers dressed in their best armor and with banners unfurled was impressive. Vásquez de Coronado had twenty-five horses and more than a few suits of armor, including one of gold gilt that he probably wore that day. One of the officers noted that "there had gathered for this expedition the most brilliant company ever assembled in the Indies to go in search of new lands."

On the next day they broke out their banners again and, with trumpets blaring, they set out for the far north on a journey that would be epic. They moved only as fast as they could move their livestock, so it was a slow pace indeed. Three officers even took their wives with them. On the advice of Marcos de Niza, the expedition made its way north up western Mexico, crossing one valley after the next, moving into dryer and more desperate territory.

Hernando de Alarcón set sail with a small armada, heading north along Mexico's west coast. The naval captain had orders to meet with the land expedition at a designated latitude, where reports could be taken and the latter expedition could be supplied before it turned inland. But the north was a great expanse and the farther the two expeditions traveled the farther they became separated, for the coast juts in a northwestern direction. Thus when Vásquez de Coronado dispatched Captain Melchor Díaz to make contact with the armada, his prolonged journey to the coast caused an unexpected delay. Meanwhile, Alarcón arrived at the designated locale and waited several weeks before deciding to leave. He left a note buried under a marked tree in case someone showed up. That these early explorers knew how to navigate vast distances with great accuracy was demonstrated when Captain Díaz found that note.

The Coronado Expedition is one of the few Spanish historical events in North America to be included in standard United States history books. The expedition traveled over three thousand miles from west-central Mexico into New Mexico, Texas, and Kansas, where, around present-day Lyons, they encountered what they called the Quivira Indians, who became known as the Wichitas. While on this journey different reconnaissance patrols crossed the Colorado River to enter California. Pedro de Tovar led another that went to the Hopi pueblos in northern Arizona and García López de Cárdenas became the first European to see the Grand Canyon, while others visited all the Indian pueblos in New Mexico. Even while camped in Kansas some minor expeditions may have entered what is today Nebraska and Missouri.

While all that sounds grand, even glorious, the actual accomplishment of getting to these places was wrought with problems and hardship. The first and most immediate disappointment was the realization that the Seven Cities of Cíbola, or the Zuni Pueblos, were not golden. When this became obvious the worried Fray Marcos de Niza sought and received permission to return to Mexico City.

The expedition's vanguard rode up to the first of the Zuni Pueblos, which the Spanish called "Hawikuh." Unknown to the travelers, they had arrived during a ceremonial. The Zunis, no doubt startled and somewhat flabbergasted at the strangers on horseback and in armor, put out cornmeal on the ground as a sign for the strangers not to pass until the ceremonial was over. The Spanish either did not understand or were not patient enough to wait, so a battle ensued. The Zunis defended themselves from behind ramparts on high ground. This strategy had worked against their traditional enemies before. Their defense was stout but eventually overcome by the more mobile and heavily armed Spanish soldiers. Vásquez de Coronado participated in the attack and was knocked unconscious and off his horse by a hail of stones.

Replica of the Kuaua murals at the ruins of Kuaua Pueblo,
Coronado State Monument, near Bernalillo. Photograph courtesy
Palace of the Governors (MNM/DCA 44483).

Word of the invaders quickly spread throughout the Pueblo world. One can imagine the discussions, rumors, and uncertainty that swept the land, especially as the Spanish vanguard continued on to Acoma, and down the Rio Puerco to the Rio Grande, somewhere below Albuquerque, where they started north. At the present site of Albuquerque they visited the pueblo of Alcanfor in the province of Tiguex. They chose one of the province's twelve pueblos for the expedition's base camp.

While there they met two representatives from Cicuye, or Pecos Pueblo, which was the largest and possibly most powerful pueblo in the area. Situated west of the Rio Grande on a rise overlooking the Pecos River from the east, Cicuye was perfectly located to trade with the nomadic Indians of the plains. As a result, the town was relatively wealthy. As a walled town, however, it demonstrated a need for caution with the nomadic trade partners who were invited to set up their fairs on the flats below the pueblo. The Apaches, also wary, set up permanent camp five miles downriver at a site presently occupied by the village of San Isidro.

The Spanish named the two emissaries Bigotes and El Turco, probably because the former had whiskers and the latter's appearance reminded them of a Turk. One of the visitors was indeed from Pecos but the other was a Pawnee, taken captive and traded to Pecos Pueblo. One or the other answered the repetitive questions about gold, silver, large cities, etc., with a familiar answer. Yes, these things existed but "más allá," much farther beyond here. The Pawnee then informed the inquisitors that his colleague was misleading them and that they had instructions to entice the Spaniards to leave the area. Nonetheless, he, who hailed from Quivira, could lead them to his rich place of birth.

Meanwhile, a soldier raped a Native woman at a nearby pueblo that the Spanish called Arenal. The Puebloans wanted justice, so Vásquez de Coronado asked tribal leaders to identify the culprit, which they proceeded to do. The man denied the accusation and his commander sided with him. Naturally, word of this incensed the afflicted pueblo, so a decision was made to exact revenge by killing some of the intruders' horses. This, in turn, enraged the Spaniards, who saw their horses as the essential means of their survival. Vásquez de Coronado quickly granted permission to Captain López de Cárdenas to lead an attack on the pueblo. The captain used that opportunity to attack and then burn the whole pueblo to the ground. Then he staked out and torched those men that he captured.

Vásquez de Coronado did not receive the news of López de Cárdenas's exploits in good spirits. The captain's actions had endangered the whole enterprise. Other pueblos joined in resistance and the Spanish responded by destroying more villages. Finally, rather than surrender, the Pueblo Indians abandoned their towns to take refuge in the mountains.

If Vásquez de Coronado was to achieve any fame he needed to act quickly. In the spring of 1541, he decided to follow the information provided by El Turco. So the expedition moved on in search of Quivira, the wealthy civilization that, he hoped, would match the riches of the Aztecs and Incas. He broke camp in Bernalillo and, with a majority of his entourage, followed El Turco from Pecos Pueblo down the Pecos River and out to the plains. There he traveled in a southeastern direction for thirty-three days, interestingly, the same amount of time that Christopher Columbus sailed from the Canary Islands before spotting land.

Vásquez de Coronado and his people always knew where they were. Almost all of his men had experience on the high seas and were familiar with vast expanses. Some members of the expedition had knowledge of the stars and understood how to calculate direction and distance. Quite naturally, they carried with them some of the same instruments that they used while at sea. Even their descriptions of the plains likened them to being at sea. When viewed from a distance the grass blowing in the breeze reminded them of waves at sea, with the buffalo as ships. They described the plains as being so flat that individuals constantly felt as if they were in a middle of a bowl. Not one person was lost on the plains during the journey.

On the thirty-third day Vásquez de Coronado realized that El Turco had been deceiving them. He called a halt to the expedition and made three decisions. First, he selected a smaller, more rapid group to continue the exploration and ordered the rest to return to the base camp. Second, he and the smaller group of about thirty men would change directions and head directly north. Finally, he ordered that El Turco be garroted for his deception.

Leaving from a spot somewhere in central Texas, the smaller group rode north, passing through the Wichita Mountains in present-day Oklahoma and into Kansas, where they came upon the widespread and numerous encampments of the Wichita Indians.

There he dispatched reconnaissance patrols to interview Natives from neighboring tribes. He also received a "foreign" Indian who claimed to have escaped another group of armored men. Many months later in Mexico City, Vásquez de Coronado learned that the foreign Indian had escaped remnants of the Hernando de Soto expedition. Soto had led an army through Florida into the Carolinas, across the Mississippi River, and up the Arkansas River to within 120 miles of Vásquez de Coronado, who was camped on the same river at the same time.

After about a month at Quivira the weary and disgruntled group began the trip back to the Rio Grande, where they arrived by October. Indian guides took them on a direct route back to New Mexico. It was a route that almost three centuries later would become the Santa Fe Trail. Back in his base camp, Vásquez de Coronado decided that he had accomplished all that he could and ordered the expedition to return to Mexico. Only the priests and their helpers could remain.

The Coronado Expedition traveled overland some nine thousand miles into the heart of North America. Vásquez de Coronado returned dejected, if not destitute, for his expedition failed to find another Mexico, a city or civilization of great wealth and advancement. On the other hand, the geographical as well as ethnological knowledge he gained was impressive. The expedition's chronicles, mostly compiled by Pedro de Castañeda, gave accurate distances, noted botanical as well as animal life, and identified different tribes, including, for the first time, an accurate description of the Apaches. In conjunction with the Soto and Alarcón northern forays, the Coronado Expedition completed a coast-to-coast exploration of North America.

Illustrated accounts of all these early explorations were published in Europe within fifteen years after Vásquez de Coronado's return to Mexico. Giovanni Batista Ramusio published a three-volume book in Venice in 1556, titled *Navigationi et viaggi. . .*, in which he recounted all of Spain's explorations to date in Italian.

Despite the knowledge gained by northern exploration, almost forty years would pass before another incursion into New Mexico would take place. The Spanish now knew that a grand and wealthy civilization did not exist in the distant north. In addition, some of Vásquez de Coronado's friends and colleagues from Nueva Galicia made a major silver discovery at a place that would be called Zacatecas. One of these men, Cristóbal de Oñate, would be the father of New Mexico's first governor. The silver discovery resulted in a rush of miners and wealth seekers into an area that the Chichimeca Indians considered their own. They resisted. The subsequent forty-year confrontation was a serious and often deadly conflict that precluded all thought of Hispanic movement farther north.

Meanwhile, Spain, with the blessing of its kings Carlos I and his son, Felipe II, initiated a series of investigations and debates over Spain's moral obligations, if any, toward the native inhabitants in America. Fray Bartolome de la Casas, a Dominican priest, argued that the Natives, as human beings with souls, required royal protection as a matter of the Crown's obligation to God. His arguments were accepted and first resulted in the "New Laws of 1542" and subsequently in a series of royal proclamations in 1573. Called *Recopilación de las leyes de los reinos de las Indias* (The Recompilation of the laws of the kingdoms of the Indies), the laws listed all the legal precedent, beginning with the laws of Ferdinand and Isabel, and concluded that the Indians were human beings and therefore subjects of the Crown of Spain.

As the Chichimeca resistance was overcome, these laws shaped how New Mexico was settled as a Spanish colony. As early as 1571 Franciscan priests, recalling that Vásquez de Coronado had left some of their brethren in "La Nueva México," suggested that an expedition needed to go north to learn the fate of those brave missionaries. The Franciscan inquiries did not fall on deaf ears, for the New Laws dictated that henceforth all expeditions would require a religious purpose and that there would be no more "conquests," but rather "pacifications" and "settlements." Use of the word "conquest," in any form, was forbidden.

In 1581, forty-one years after Vásquez de Coronado's grand army left western Mexico, a small band led by Fray Agustín Rodríquez left the village of Santa Barbara in north-central Mexico. Father Rodríquez took with him two other priests, a nine-soldier escort led by the elderly captain Francisco Sánchez Chamuscado, and between sixteen and twenty Indians. They took a new route into New Mexico, traveling north over known territory to the Conchos River, and following it north to the Rio Grande, or as they called it then, the Rio Bravo del Norte or, more commonly, Rio del Norte. They progressed upriver through the pass, El Paso, into New Mexico, where they left the river for a shortcut across a barren stretch that would come to be called the "Route of the Dead Man" or "Jornada del Muerto." They traveled to their destination, the land of the Pueblo People, with little hardship and immediately confirmed what they had suspected. The first Franciscans had been killed, martyred from their point of view. They had already learned that one, Fray Juan de Padilla, had returned to Quivira, where he was killed, because the priest's Portuguese servant, Andrés de Campo, witnessed the death and with the help of his dog returned to Mexico to tell the tale. Another priest, Fray Luís de Ubeda, suffered a similar fate, probably at Pecos Pueblo.

Undaunted, the small band explored west to Acoma Pueblo and

then on to the Zuni region. They then returned to cross the Rio Grande Valley and explore the Galisteo villages. The people at San Marcos Pueblo, which the Spaniards called Malpartida and which is now in ruins, told the explorers that they were only two days' march from the cows on the plains and that the herds came as close as some twenty miles from the pueblo. The Natives volunteered to help guide the curious Spaniards to the herds, so they headed off to the plains. They crossed the Pecos River and headed northeast until they came upon the Canadian River, which they followed farther east into the plains. There they spent two weeks and saw buffalo "so large that when seen in the midst of a plain they resemble ships at sea or carts on land." Like Vásquez de Coronado's expedition before them, they were impressed enough by these new "shaggy cows" to name the area of their travels Cíbola, "the land of the buffalo."

After returning from the plains, Fray Juan de Santa María was sent back to convey news of the expedition, but he too suffered the fate of the earlier priests when "Manga" Indians killed him south of Socorro. After a little more exploration the expedition's leadership decided to split up. The remaining two Franciscans, Rodríquez and Francisco López, elected to stay and work among the Pueblo people. Captain Sánchez Chamuscado led the rest of the expedition south on their return journey. The old captain never completed the journey, for he died of a stomach ailment after reaching the Conchos River. The survivors made it to Santa Barbara in April of 1582 with the news that one priest was missing and the other two had stayed in New Mexico.

The report of the Rodríquez-Chamuscado expedition generated an excited interest in further exploration to the north. The missionaries could not be left alone. They needed to be rescued. Within seven months Fray Antonio de Beltrán and Antonio de Espejo led the rescue mission north. At Puaray, in the Tiguex province, they quickly learned that friars Rodríquez and López had been killed. That news, along with the deaths of Vásquez de Coronado's eight priests and the confirmation of Santa María's death, meant that a total of eleven Franciscans had been martyred in the north.

Beltrán and Espejo split up, with Espejo visiting various pueblos, including the Hopis to the west, where he heard stories of rich rivers.

Father Beltrán led the remaining men back down the Rio Grande. Espejo followed a few months later, taking the Pecos River south.

The interest in New Mexico no longer centered on rumored rich civilizations. The only gold and silver there would have to be located and extracted from the ground. The Pueblo Indians, however, had become even more of an attraction to the Franciscans, who now counted their martyred brethren in the province.

The viceroy in Mexico City as well as the king of Spain weighed the possibilities of settling the area, while any number of would-be leaders clamored for the opportunity to win glory and royal favor. The Franciscans also argued for movement into New Mexico. Franciscan blood sanctified the very ground of this distant place. This was a holy opportunity that the king could hardly ignore. Indeed, the Pueblo Indians were prime targets for conversion by the sons of St. Francis. The Pueblo people were sedentary and, as such, the missionaries knew that they would be easier to convert. In New Mexico the work of conversion to the Holy Faith, or *Santa Fe*, could be done in earnest. Nomadic peoples, those who constantly moved around, presented more difficult targets for conversion. The Crown agreed, but not before some adventurers, in anticipation to the royal action, made their own history.

International competition and intrigue perhaps motivated the Crown to want more information about the far north. In part, this competition stimulated European as well as American exploration for centuries. Portugal and Spain were the first to compete for the quickest route to Asia. After encountering the Americas, a waterway through the landmass became paramount. Which European country would be the first to find what the Spanish called the "Straights of Anián," or the English called the "Northwest Passage"? Spain's greatest competitor, commercially as well as religiously, became England. The infamous, from the Spanish point of view, Francis Drake unofficially sailed and raided Spanish ports for England's Queen Elizabeth I.

Drake already had a sordid reputation in Spain when he navigated through the Magellan Straights and into the Pacific Ocean, the "Mar del Sud" or "Sur"—the South Sea. He then sailed up the west coast of South America to Mexico, raiding settlements and attacking Spanish merchantmen along the way. After Mexico he headed up the California coast to regroup before he completed his circumnavigation of the globe to reappear in England. Spanish officialdom immediately speculated that he had found the heretofore unknown waterway and this necessitated some high-level planning.

Historians later learned that he left Mexico and sailed up the west coast to a bay north of San Francisco Bay, where he rested and refurbished his ship, *The Golden Hind*. He then embarked west to cross the Pacific Ocean to the Indian Ocean and then sailed around Africa to complete his historic trip.

The possibility that the Spanish Crown's decision to settle New Mexico was influenced by this suspected British discovery of the route to China, as well as the church's argument to convert the sedentary Indians, and also rumors of mineral wealth waiting for discovery in New Mexico is plausible but unproven. Nonetheless, Spain did take a renewed interest in establishing a settlement far beyond the Spanish northern frontier line in north-central Mexico.

The first official correspondence suggesting such a venture came to Mexico City as early as April 1583. The viceroy asked for candidates for the venture. Antonio de Espejo, who had already been to New Mexico, and six other would-be governors petitioned for the job. The competition was stringent, political, and hard fought. One candidate lost out when unsubstantiated charges surfaced that he had poisoned his wife. The viceroy did not select a winner before he was replaced and his successor decided to renew the competition.

∞

Meanwhile, perhaps displaying the impatience of conquistadores a generation before, or trying to emulate the success of Hernán Cortés, who himself began the conquest of Mexico without royal approval, two illegal expeditions left northern Mexico for New Mexico.

The first of these was Nuevo León's lieutenant governor Gaspar Castaño de Sosa, who, with his followers, was described by the viceroy as "outlaws, criminals, and murderers" as well as illegal slave traders. Castaño de Sosa took with him virtually the whole population from the village of Almadén, today's Monclova, in the state of Coahuila. The illegal colony of nearly two hundred people and no priests packed their wagons and left for New Mexico in the summer of 1589. They followed the Rodríquez-Chamuscado route until they diverted to follow the Pecos River north.

The illegal band forcibly subjugated Pecos Pueblo and then visited the other pueblos, alienating them as well. Castaño de Sosa gambled that his success would win royal favor. The problem with his bootleg attempt at settlement was that the venture not only lacked royal approval, but it in fact flaunted his king, Felipe II, who had enacted laws prohibiting these types of expeditions. Castaño de Sosa never had a chance to succeed, for the viceroy did not hesitate to dispatch a squad of soldiers under the command of Juan Morlete to go north and arrest the whole group. Morlete found Castaño de Sosa's party at the Keresan pueblo Santo Domingo, where the renegade leader was arrested, put in chains, and, with the entire colony, returned south to face trial. In 1593, Castaño de Sosa was found guilty of crimes against the Crown and sentenced to an exile of military service on a Manila galleon in the Philippines. While serving his sentence he was killed in a Chinese slave uprising on board a galleon sailing for the Moluccas Islands in the South Pacific Ocean.

Some historians have attributed Castaño de Sosa's failed attempt to colonize New Mexico to reasons other than to achieve a fait accompli and subsequent glory. One of these theories suggests that his colony was actually an attempt by people who continued to secretly practice their Jewish religion to move away from Spanish officialdom. However, the trials themselves reveal no such reasons.

A few years later, in 1593, a second, even more blatantly illegal expedition traveled to New Mexico. Two shadowy characters named Francisco Leyva de Bonilla and Antonio Gutiérrez de Humaña went north with no pretensions for settlement. Almost inexplicably they went in search of riches. They explored and apparently alienated those with whom they came in contact. Finding nothing of interest in New Mexico, where they spent a year based at San Ildefonso Pueblo, they decided to go onto the plains in search of Quivira. They traveled across the plains to somewhere around present-day Wichita, Kansas, or maybe near the junction of the Arkansas and Walnut rivers in southern Kansas. There they met a fate far worse than Castaño de Sosa's, and thanks to an account of the expedition's lone survivor, a Mexican Indian servant named Jusepe Gutiérrez, and subsequent evidence, the story can be told with reasonable certainty.

They had retraced Vásquez de Coronado's return route from Quivira, moving in the opposite direction, crossing two rivers and traveling eighteen days. They came upon an Indian settlement so large that it took them many days to travel through it. The people lived in houses built with poles and straw and they grew corn, squash, and beans. From there they proceeded north and on the third day a dispute broke out that resulted in the stabbing death of Leyva de Bonilla by Gutiérrez de Humaña. Until this point Leyva de Bonilla had been the expedition's leader. With their leader dead many of the Indian servants fled. The rest of the expedition perished when attacked by Plains Indians. Only Jusepe survived to tell the tale.

∞

Back in Mexico in 1595, Viceroy Luis de Velasco chose Juan de Oñate to lead the legal, government-sanctioned settlement of New Mexico. But before Oñate could fulfill his obligation, a new viceroy, Gaspar de Zúñiga y Acevedor, the count of Monterey, replaced Velasco and he decided to reexamine Oñate's application while considering a different applicant. In 1598, after years of delay and time-consuming official inspections, Oñate's expedition was allowed to leave north-central Mexico to make history.

Gaspar Pérez de Villagrá, around fifty-five years old, from the original edition of his Historia de la Nueva Mexico *(1610). Original in the Fray Angélico Chávez Library. Courtesy Palace of the Governors (MNM/DCA 152680).*

CHAPTER FOUR

An Island in the Wilderness

New Mexico Settled

ᘒᘒ

Juan de Oñate is New Mexico's most controversial figure. He is New Mexico's first governor and as such deserves credit for establishing the first permanent Spanish colony in the region. This was no small accomplishment, for the experience of setting up an inland colony so far from the rest of the Spanish expansion was very unusual at the time. Yet, this singular achievement became obscured by Oñate's own estimate of his accomplishments, because of reports by many of his disgruntled colonists, and by his own government's condemnation of his activities.

Juan de Oñate was the son of don Cristóbal de Oñate, who had sailed to Nueva España in 1524 and compiled a positive record serving the Crown on the frontier for many years before he became one of the so-called "big four." He, along with Juan de Tolosa, Diego de Ibarra, and Baltasar Treviño, discovered and opened the silver lodes in and around Zacatecas. Juan de Oñate, born relatively late in his father's life, also entered the royal service and by the time of his application to settle New Mexico, had compiled two decades of experience on the frontier. He had a wealth of experience in mining as well as fighting the Chichimecas and other Indians. He also inherited his father's mining enterprises, which made him a wealthy man. His service, wealth, willingness, and not-too-demanding application won him the job.

Oñate offered to recruit two hundred fully equipped men whose salaries he would pay. He would also contract for supplies and livestock, which amounted to over four thousand head, including cattle, sheep, goats, horses, etc. He asked the government to provide funds for five priests and a lay brother, some pieces of artillery, and a six-year loan of six thousand pesos. He requested the titles of governor and captain-general and, if he succeeded in settling New Mexico, he wanted the honorific title of *adelantado*. Upon his acceptance, he received the right of *encomienda*, the assignation of a large number of Indians for three generations. He also received the authority to grant encomiendas to his followers.

After many delays the expedition left Santa Barbara in north-central New Spain on 25 January 1598. Oñate had with him 129 soldiers, their families and servants, plus other undocumented people, including Mexican Indian carriers. He also had eight Franciscan priests and two lay brothers, eighty-three wagons, and over seven thousand head of livestock. At least one of the priests was a relative while his two nephews, Vicente and Juan de Zaldívar, served as sergeant major and camp master (*maese de campo*) respectively. He brought his young son along but left his wife and a daughter in Mexico. In total, an estimated 850 people started north.

One of the more interesting and noteworthy members of the expedition was Gaspar Pérez de Villagrá (Villagrán), whom Oñate recruited to be a captain and legal advisor. Like Oñate, he was born to Spanish parents in Mexico. He attended the University of Salamanca, where he majored in law. While he deserted Oñate after eighteen months, he and his leader would become famous because of the 1610 publication of his epic poem extolling the virtues of the governor as he colonized New Mexico. The book-length poem, *La Historia de la Nueva México*, has become a prime, if tenuous, source of information for the initial months of Oñate's northern enterprise.

The expedition also included some veterans from the Castaño de Sosa expedition and at least one person from the Rodríquez-Chamuscado expedition. These people would be of assistance with the route. Nevertheless, Oñate deviated from the known route to take a more direct passage through the Chihuahua desert and the sand dunes there. They traveled over incredibly harsh, arid, and hostile territory for almost four months before they reached the Rio Grande, where parched men and animals plunged into the water to quench their thirst. Some of the horses actually drank themselves to death. This would be a necessary and fitting incident that people who live in the area would understand for centuries to come. The abundant game, pleasant river bottom, and the fact that the colony had made it to El Paso del Norte, the northern pass into New Mexico, justified Oñate's decision to stop for a much-needed rest and to give thanks. Oñate also used the occasion to claim all the land beyond the pass for his king and God. Clearly, that spot, about twenty miles downriver from the City of El Paso, somewhere around present-day San Elizario, Texas, is "*la toma*," the spot for the taking of possession. For some people in the Hispanic community of the United States, this location is the equivalent of Plymouth Rock.

After a rest, the colony left the encampment of that pleasant location without a recorded complaint. They moved north through the pass and continued up the Rio Grande. Perhaps these people shared an indelible sense of adventure prevalent in the world during those days. They knew what waited for them in New Mexico. It was not another Mexico City but a series of rock and mud Indian villages. And among those villages they would make a home for themselves. From that basis, the missionaries would spread out among the Indians and begin what they believed to be the work of God and their king: to convert souls to Christianity, which to them meant the Catholic Church. The expedition owed its existence to the arguments of the clergy. King Felipe II took his obligation seriously, begun three generations earlier by his great-grandparents *Los Reyes Católicos*, Ferdinand and Isabel, who had received from Pope Alexander VI the rights to explore, settle, and benefit from the Americas. That obligation, codified in the New Laws and Recopilaciones, dictated that Oñate, whether or not he lived up to the role, was leading an expedition in fulfillment of the Crown's sacred duty. New Mexico was to be settled as a missionary field.

*The centerpiece of a banner brought to New Mexico by
Juan de Oñate in 1598. A depiction of Our Lady of the Remedies.
Original in the collections of the Archdiocese of Santa Fe.
Photograph courtesy Palace of the Governors (MNM/DCA 160407).*

The tediously slow progress up the Rio Grande Valley became
even slower when the colony came upon the villages of the Pueblo
Indians. One of the first of these was the Piro pueblo that the Spanish
called Socorro, from the word "succor" or "to help," for the food that
the inhabitants supplied the newcomers. Oñate, impatient to travel
faster, went ahead with an advance contingent. By mid-June, Oñate

chose an upriver village called Ohke to be his headquarters. He re-named the pueblo, north of present-day Española, San Juan de los Caballeros. There, he established the first Spanish capital of the "king-dom of New Mexico."

Within a couple of years his capital would be called San Gabriel. Historians have speculated that the governor moved his colony across the river to a different village, called Yunque Yunque. However, some recent speculations are that the governor renamed his original capital and never moved at all.

As soon as the colony had settled in a group of vacated Pueblo Indian buildings, Oñate began to have problems. He felt that he needed to explore the lands, especially to find the elusive waterway that connected the North and South seas. He also wanted to search for signs of extractive wealth—gold and silver. Exploration diverted atten-tion away from the basic work needed to survive. The arrival of Jusepe Gutiérrez, an Indian from Mexico who survived the Gutiérrez de Humaña and Leyva de Bonilla debacle, further wetted Oñate's appetite for exploration.

The Plains Indians had held Jusepe Gutiérrez captive for three years before he escaped. He was an excellent source of information about the area. Oñate immediately sent Vicente de Zaldívar on an expedition to explore the plains with Jusepe's guidance. Oñate, on the other hand, traveled south to visit the new mission area on the east side of the Manzano Mountains, but he suddenly decided to turn west and look for the South Sea. Meanwhile, Juan de Zaldívar was left in charge at San Juan until his brother returned from the plains. At that time, Juan had orders that he was to catch up with Oñate.

Vicente de Zaldívar had a fairly uneventful trip on the plains. He vainly tried to herd some buffalo back to San Juan but learned that the animals were not susceptible to such treatment. According to plan, Juan de Zaldívar took a small contingent to find Oñate. While in route he stopped at Acoma Pueblo, where he was ambushed and killed, along with some others in the group. Upon hearing of the attack, somewhere in present-day Arizona, Oñate cut short his trip. He was worried that the actions of the Acoma Indians could be part of a greater resistance and that he had left his capital in jeopardy. When he returned to Zuni he was surprised to hear that his fellow Basque, Pérez de Villagrá, had been rescued, nearly frozen and starved to death. Pérez de Villagrá had been sent south in pursuit of four deserters, whom he caught just north of Santa Barbara. Per orders he garroted two of them, while the other two avoided the same fate by escaping. He, too, was trying to catch up to Oñate when his horse fell into an Indian animal trap and left him on foot in a blizzard. He was found at present-day El Morro next to the pond at the base of the cliff.

The governor quickly returned to his headquarters, where he gave the job of revenge and of setting an example to Juan's brother, Vicente de Zaldívar. The subsequent battle at Acoma combined bravery, endurance, and treachery on both sides, and is a source of emotion to the present. Ultimately, despite the refusal of many Acoma men to surrender, the pueblo was defeated and burnt to the ground. Many of the surviving defenders were taken prisoner and tried at Santo Domingo Pueblo. Oñate insisted on presiding over the trials and he found all brought before him guilty of rebellion. All the prisoners were sentenced to servitude. A group of women were sent to Mexico. Many of the men were physically punished before being given to some of Oñate's followers to become servants.

The physical punishment has become a source of contention. Many historians have written that Oñate ordered that each mature male have a foot cut off. But recent research has indicated that there is no evidence of this happening and that, at most, the prisoners lost some toes. This latter theory makes sense, for losing toes rather than a whole foot left the prisoners useful as servants. Nevertheless, the pueblo of Acoma suffered a horrible defeat. Oñate used that pueblo as an example to other pueblos. Whether his strategy worked or not is subject to debate. Acoma was reoccupied and functioning within a year.

The Spanish colony's initial months in New Mexico were not much different from the experiences of early English attempts at colonization on the East Coast. Along with resistant Indians and a very harsh first winter, Oñate had problems with the clergy and his own people, who as noted above, began deserting the colonial effort. The settlers had become so disillusioned that by the fall of 1601, scarcely two dozen people remained loyal to him and this despite reinforcements of eighty new settlers and seven Franciscans. The disappointedly small supplement of new settlers had arrived on Christmas Eve, 1600. By the end of 1601

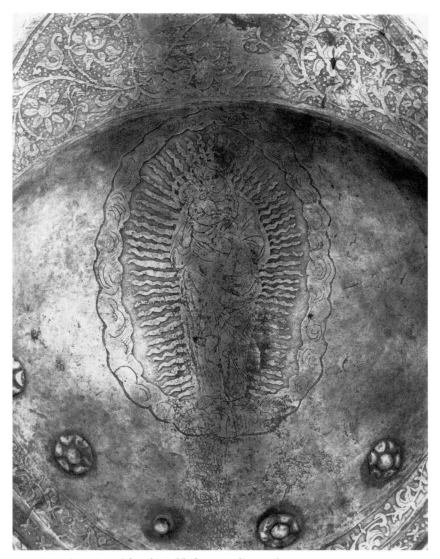

Morrión, *Spanish colonial helmet, Italian style, ca. 1600,*
with an image of Our Lady of the Immaculate Conception.
Original in the collections of the Palace of the Governors.
Photograph courtesy Palace of the Governors (MNM/DCA 177906).

possibly as many as two thirds of the colony had deserted. Oñate executed some of the detractors. Those who successfully escaped criticized his management of the colony and those complaints would eventually result in his removal, trial, and conviction. Even his nephew Vicente de Zaldívar's 1603 trip to Spain, where he pled Oñate's case, fell on deaf ears.

Oñate left New Mexico in 1609 under less than desirable circumstances. He would spend the rest of his life trying to rectify his record. His reputation, to this day, has remained a source of controversy. However, before he left New Mexico he did achieve some milestones. He traversed the territory west to the Hopi pueblos and then south to the Gulf of California, then called the Sea of Cortés, the sight of which was probably his happiest moment as governor. On his return trip he stopped at the familiar site early Spanish maps call *el Tanque*, now known as El Morro, where he carved his name and date along with the information that he was returning from the South Sea. In 1601, he was the first to take a caravan of wagons, along with about sixty men, across the plains to Quivira and back. The return trip, following Vásquez de Coronado's old route, took fifty-nine days. Almost unnoticed in his historical legacy is the story of Captain Juan Martínez de Montoya, who came to New Mexico in charge of that group of eighty reinforcements in late 1600. The captain "populated" and "established the plaza of Santa Fe" sometime around 1607 under Oñate's authority. Most significantly, the colony begun by Oñate survived its harsh beginnings. Whether he recognized its importance or not, New Mexico's first governor successfully colonized the area.

Upon Oñate's recall, the viceroy named Martínez de Montoya his temporary replacement but the captain declined the position. He had served the required five years and had no intention of staying longer than necessary in New Mexico. Both the captain and his governor left New Mexico in 1609. They left with the information that Pedro de Peralta, the newly appointed governor, was on his way north. Whether they met on the trail is an intriguing question that has never been answered.

Pedro de Peralta arrived in New Mexico in early 1610. He came armed with instructions to locate the northern water passage and secure a good port that could be defended against the enemies and commercial competitors of Spain. Although Spain was gaining knowledge contrary

Juan Martínez de Montoya documents opened to one of two places where he relates that he "created the plaza of Santa Fe." Photograph by Blair Clark. Courtesy of the author.

to such beliefs, the Straits of Anián and other myths still prevailed in the minds of Europeans. Oñate's experience was reflected in more mundane matters, for Peralta's instructions also mandated that he relocate the kingdom's capital to a more central location and away from any Indian pueblo. The fulfillment of this instruction resulted in the 1610 establishment of the Villa of Santa Fe as the new capital. Governmental as well as religious buildings were constructed in accordance with the law. Today, some four centuries later, Santa Fe remains the capital and the remnants of the first governmental buildings exist as the Palace of the Governors.

∞

Hispanic population increased up and down the Rio Grande Valley, while the clergy reinforced and expanded their missions among the various pueblos, where they began their work of converting, instructing, and building new missions. As did Oñate, Peralta had his problems. The Franciscans believed that the colony existed to serve their work while the governors felt that the colony itself had priority. This difference of emphasis resulted in what historian France V. Scholes called a struggle between church and state. And the rift was exacerbated by some overzealous priests who faced off against governors who, more times than not, were less-than-quality governmental officials themselves. Some of the father custodians, or head Franciscans, dealt as harshly with their own brethren as they did with lay people. At the same time, many, if not most, of the governors realized that their assignment to New Mexico was akin to political exile and so had little motivation to be sterling civil servants. While the priests and governors were not always confronting each other, their differences born out of their priorities were always close to igniting. A father custodian who, it was discovered, was not even a priest, even excommunicated Governor Peralta. The settlers and especially the Indians suffered the most from this conflict.

As late as the 1620s Fray Jerónimo de Zárate Salmerón wrote about the mythical kingdoms that circled New Mexico. He wrote of places called Tidan, Chillescas, Guismanes, and Aburcos. He wondered whether they had been partially Christianized by some celestial miracle. Possibly the real calling to the missionaries in New Mexico was to complete the miracle.

Another friar embellished on what he heard from priests who had preceded him in New Mexico. In a report presented to his king, Felipe IV, in 1630, Fray Alonso de Benavides described the colony, the country, each of the pueblos being administered, and then wrote about a barefoot Trappist Franciscan nun, María de Agreda. The nun, he claimed, had bilocated to New Mexico to direct the Indians to seek instruction from the blue-clad friars. Upon his return to Spain he even visited the famous cloistered nun to have her confirm his interpretation of what New Mexicans would call "the Lady in Blue," in reference to the color of her habit. Zárate Salmerón, who constructed the first church at Jémez Pueblo, wrote an earlier *relación*, on which the bishop in Mexico added a notation that mentioned the Lady in Blue as evidence of God's approval for the missionaries' work.

For some years the Franciscans were fairly successful and the colony seemed to be progressing. Missionaries, with the help of their Native American communities, built missions—Zia (ca. 1613), Jémez (1621–22), Pecos (ca. 1622), and Acoma (1629–41), among others, sprang up in rapid order. In 1625 Fray Benavides received the appointment of father custodian and was the first priest to arrive in New Mexico vested with the powers of the office of the Inquisition. While he found Inquisition-related complaints nonessential and hardly worth acknowledging, thus setting the tone for that High Holy Tribunal for the rest of New Mexico's history, he did become significant for other reasons. First, he initiated and oversaw the construction of San Miguel Mission in the Barrio de Analco district of Santa Fe. This church still stands today and has been mistakenly described as the oldest church in the United States. Analco, the neighborhood in which it was built, was on the south side of the Santa Fe River, opposite the plaza, which was surrounded by the presidio and official buildings on the north side of the river. The name is a Nahuatl term that means "other side of the water" and is evidence to the existence of Nahuatl speakers, Mexican Indians and their descendents, who moved to New Mexico as servants and guides who lived in Analco from the time of the first expeditions.

Father Benavides brought with him a small statue that he most likely purchased in Mexico. The statue was Nuestra Señora de la Asunción (Our Lady of the Assumption), whose name was quickly changed to Nuestra Señora del Rosario, Our Lady of the Rosary. The statue of Mary soon received the more popular appellation of "La Conquistadora" or the more formal "La Conquista," which has been incorrectly translated as "the Conqueror." The name came out of church lexicon and iconography of the Mother of God being able to bring people together out of her love for them, as exhibited by her suffering and love for her Son. Her method is a conquest of love. So,

"Our Lady of the Rosary, the Unifier" would become an icon in New Mexico. In the twentieth century the Vatican proclaimed her the official patroness of New Mexico. Within six years of her arrival in New Mexico a confraternity in her name had formed and become active.

Like the early expeditions that kept journals or *relaciones*, some of the early Franciscans wrote reports about their new assignments. Father Benavides wrote perhaps the most important and subsequently most published *memorial*. Benavides wrote his report in conjunction with a trip that he took to Spain in 1629 to recruit more priests and, it appears, to have himself appointed New Mexico's first bishop.

Benavides's aforementioned report was presented to the king in 1630. He evidently was as good a promoter as he was a writer, for he received an invitation to send a revised memorial to the pope. He completed this task in 1634. Both memorials have been translated into English and are available today. While Father Benavides never returned to New Mexico, instead receiving an appointment to India, his work did result in the assignment of more priests to his former custody and the establishment of a long-term commitment for royal support of the Franciscans.

At around the same time that Fray Benavides was in New Mexico, a settler known as "El Alemán," or "the German," got into trouble and was arrested and jailed in Santa Fe. He escaped and made a desperate attempt to flee south, hoping to lose his pursuers once he reached the settlements of north-central Mexico. A posse followed after him. He was tracked south past the Piro pueblos and then onto the well-known shortcut that took a more direct southern route across the desert behind the Fra Cristóbal Mountains. The shortcut, while dangerous, avoided a time-consuming bend in the Rio Grande. The escaped prisoner failed in his attempt to cross the desert alone. His pursuers found his body on that barren stretch. From that day on the dangerous shortcut became known as the Jornada del Muerto, or Journey of the Dead Man, in reference to the unfortunate German fugitive.

∞

The quality of New Mexico's civil leaders, all appointed from outside the area, ran the gamut, primarily from mediocre to bad. One governor,

Luís de Rosas, was assassinated, stabbed to death for his shenanigans. Two others were brought before the Inquisition in Mexico City, one for legitimate reasons, the other for conjured charges grown out of political motives. Any New Mexican facing charges before the Inquisition would be summoned to Mexico City to stand trial and if found culpable, would receive the tribunal's sentence. A few New Mexicans suffered the process and only one was found guilty. The others, it turns out, were charged because of rumors and innuendoes born out of personal and sometimes political rivalries. The process itself was punishment enough.

Governor Diego Dionosio Peñalosa was the one individual to be found guilty. He was sentenced to walk the streets of Mexico City in a special robe, holding a candle, and with a sign proclaiming his transgressions. He was exiled from all Spanish territories, including Spain. Peñalosa did indeed have a sordid history. Before his appointment to New Mexico he had been involved in a murder in Perú and as a convicted felon was transferred in chains aboard a ship to Mexico. He miraculously survived when his ship wrecked during a storm. Somehow he made it to Mexico City, where he befriended the viceroy, who shipped him far out of town with an appointment to the position of governor of New Mexico.

Upon his arrival in New Mexico he immediately alienated the missionaries as well as the lay people. His audacity, high-handed ways, and his own words eventually attracted enemies and, in turn, the Inquisition. He even fabricated a report of an expedition out onto the plains that he claimed he led. When confronted about his affronts to the Franciscans in 1664, he remarked:

> If the custodian excommunicated me, I would hang him
> or garrote him immediately, and if the Pontiff came here
> and wanted to excommunicate me or actually did so, I
> would hang the Pontiff, because in this kingdom, I am
> the prince and supreme magistrate.

Aside from being New Mexico's most notorious colonial governor, the tale of Peñalosa is worthy of note because of the influence that he would have on New Mexico's history. After his sentence and exile from Spanish territory he traveled to France, where he exaggerated the wealth of northern New Spain as one who had been there. He wanted to convince the king of France to allow him to lead an expedition to New Mexico from the Gulf of Mexico. He argued that under his leadership France could gain this rich area from the Spanish.

While Peñalosa made his arguments in France, René-Robert Cavelier, Sieur de La Salle, arrived to make a similar plea to his king. La Salle had recently completed an epic journey down the Mississippi River to its mouth and then returned back up the river, eventually going through Canada and on to France. He argued for the establishment of a French colony at the river's mouth to effectively give France a claim to the center of North America. The two arguments dovetailed nicely and quite naturally the king chose a Frenchman to lead the expedition. Sieur de La Salle received permission to execute his plan and the result of La Salle's famous expedition had a definite impact in New Mexico, as will be seen in the next chapter.

∞

Along with its governance and religion, Spain brought people and its culture to the region. The colony was never heavily populated. Nor did the settlers seem overly concerned about adverse relations with the Pueblo Indians. From the very first settlements, some individuals chose to move away from established towns. For example, one of Oñate's colonists took his family to live among the inhabitants of Santa Clara Pueblo, where he raised sheep without fear and in peace.

Even the site of Santa Fe had been settled by a few Spanish agriculturalists before the locale became an official village. The people, to be sure, had to be self-sufficient in that they had to raise crops and animals, construct their own houses out of stone or adobe, haul water, create irrigation systems, and be prepared to defend themselves from attack by nomadic raiders who surrounded the area. Clearly, the Spanish system, if not attitude, allowed them to take advantage of their Pueblo Indian neighbors. Like all societies, it seems the farther away from authority people are, the less attentive they become to the rules and laws under which they live. The Spanish institutions, although many still had their origins in medieval law, actually reflected the Crown's efforts to protect the Indians. Yet, in practice, quite the opposite often occurred.

The system of the *encomienda* is an example of this concept. Simply put, the encomienda was intended to be a system that both rewarded settlers for their service and protected Indians. The recipient or *encomendero* had the right to receive Indian labor, which could amount to so many work hours or the product thereof. In exchange for this labor the settler was charged with arranging for religious instruction for, as well as the protection of, the Indians from whose labor he or she benefited. In addition, the law was specific to the point of delineating hours per day for labor and for proper rest time, nourishment, and time required to meet other survival responsibilities. In other words, the system was intended to benefit the laborer as well as the encomendero and not to be a detriment to either. The idea of encomienda was born out of the peonage system in Spain and throughout Europe, where the lord protected and provided for vassals who worked his land. Yet, with few exceptions the encomienda became an institution that systematically abused the Pueblo people.

Spain also assured the survival of Pueblo Indians by giving each of the pueblos an official grant of land consisting of four leagues by four leagues (one league measured about 2.6 miles in New Mexico and Mexico, so a grant represented about 100 square miles), the center of which was measured from the pueblo's plaza. This practice was abused in many cases and especially at those pueblos located along the Rio Grande, as Spanish settlers illegally but effectively encroached upon the Pueblos' lands. The missionaries saw themselves as protectors of the Indians and constantly complained about the abuses. Yet they, in their own religious zeal, did not tolerate or appreciate the Native customs, all of which had religious significance.

Probably the greatest complaint about abuses resulted from laws that allowed Spanish combatants to make slaves of or, at least, put into servitude those who resisted them. These "wartime" captives became household servants as well as the forced labor for sweatshops producing materials for trade south. Governors ran many of these small factories. They were resentful of their assignments to New Mexico, if not their low pay, and attempted to enrich themselves through illegal means. More times than not the labor force was not captured in combat but merely taken or, as became the custom, obtained in trade at one of the trade fairs.

The trade fairs provide an interesting example of how strict adherence to the law backfired. The fairs had been held even before the Spanish moved into the area. As mentioned earlier, certain pueblos such as Pecos, Taos, and those in the Abiquiu area that existed on the frontier of the Pueblo sedentary world and the nomadic world of various tribes, held annual trade fairs outside their respective pueblos. At that time a truce would be called and business conducted. The Spanish adapted to this system, which by the eighteenth century had become a normal part of life in New Mexico.

Part of that trade always had been in human beings. Many of the people who would come to be called *genízaros* in New Mexico were descendants of captives traded into New Mexican society at the trade fairs. Such trade was illegal under Spanish law and the king and the viceroy wanted human trade in New Mexico to stop. As early as 1694 Governor Vargas tried to obey the letter of the law by stopping the trade in Pawnee children. At the time, the Navajos took annual trips on foot from their land in Arizona and New Mexico to raid Pawnee villages in present-day Nebraska! To undertake such a long journey to take prisoners, preferably youths, for trade in New Mexico indicates that the Navajos thought that the activity was beneficial to them. However, the governor decided to obey his viceroy's order and rode up to the Taos trade fair that year to put a halt to the activity. His very presence at the fair indicated the seriousness with which he took the task. Upon hearing that the Spanish would no longer participate in trading for Pananas, as the Spanish called the Pawnees, the Navajos reacted by summarily killing every one of the prisoners in front of the governor. The governor, somewhat taken aback, then wrote his viceroy with the story and requested advice as to what the king would suggest under the circumstance. The reply ordered him to allow human trading as before.

Slaves or hostages also included Hispanics who were taken in raids and usually traded back in the fairs. Human trade was complex.

All these systems and abuses led to charges and countercharges that in turn led to exacerbated tensions and violence. More than one governor was excommunicated, tantamount to condemnation to hell, by the Franciscan prelate while governors and their men put more than one priest in jail. Leaders of various Indian tribes as well as the Spanish leadership became weary of each other. As can be imagined, such conflicts permeated society, including the Pueblo Indians. Survival was hard enough.

The area of the upper Rio Grande Valley continued to be a sedentary enclave in the middle of a nomadic world. The sedentary people had to be self-sufficient. For the Spanish, distance from Mexico precluded dependency on the south. The expectation of receiving necessaries through trade did not exist. Eventually, New Mexicans came to relish their independence.

The climate in the far north was much colder than farther south and even colder than in the present. Winters lasted longer and temperatures regularly dropped to zero degrees Fahrenheit and below and stayed at that level in the Rio Grande Valley. The summer's heat became a mixed blessing. The dry climate determined that dry farming and extensive irrigation systems had to be carefully maintained, for dependency on the pueblos for food quickly faded as the Pueblo population decreased.

Of course, personal security was a priority. As has happened throughout history, the nomadic peoples raided the sedentary peoples. The severity of this inevitable activity of raiding for food eventually curtails as societies learn to trade. Apache, Navajo, and Ute people traded before the Spanish arrived. Now the Spanish traded as well. As noted earlier, everyone adapted to existing trading patterns. So this early form of syncretism, the mixing of cultures, took place initially among the Pueblo people, who then mixed with the various nomadic peoples surrounding them. Then the Spanish joined the process. Pecos, as mentioned, had been a trading center long before the Spanish arrived. The Pecos fair continued as always on the plain below the east wall. Natural enemies who became trading partners still kept their guard up.

By 1680 the Hispanic population had grown to between two and three thousand people, who were mostly, but not entirely, living in the Rio Arriba, that area upriver from the Jémez Mountain lava flow called La Bajada, "the lowering," in reference to the drop in elevation from the capital at Santa Fe. The Pueblo Indian population had decreased from a high estimate of eighty thousand people to around thirty thousand and possibly lower. Life was not easy. The various cultures continued to survive but not without changes and challenges. Their religions survived but not without many problems. The disruption among the Pueblo people began with the arrival of the Navajo people, around fifty years before the Spanish. The Pueblos thus suffered two shocks to their system of life within a short time span. For Hispanics too, survival was problematic. Still, cultures and the people in those cultures persisted. If anything, New Mexicans proved to be survivors. Spanish institutions were introduced into the area. The many cultures did what all cultures do: borrow what is beneficial to them and discard that which is not useful.

Syncretism, the mixing of cultures, had begun but not all was well. Spanish abuses of their own laws and zealous priests with no tolerance for native customs slowed the process of learning to live together. As early as 1650, the lesson of Acoma had been forgotten, for a group of several southern pueblos between Cochiti and Isleta conspired with Apaches to rebel against the Spanish. The plot was discovered and nine of the Pueblo leaders were hanged. Many others received punishment.

A subsequent drought that began in 1666 and lasted five years worsened the plight of the Pueblo Indians. Weakened from lack of food, burdened to work more for less, subject to famine and increasing attacks from equally desperate Apache Indians, the Pueblo religious leaders clearly saw that the blame rested with the Spanish, who prohibited them from attending to their gods, who now punished them.

Another rebellion was planned among the pueblos along the eastside of the Manzano Mountains. The leader of the intended insurrection was a native of Abó Pueblo named Esteban Clemente, who was described as the governor of the Salinas ("saline," for the salt lakes close by) and the Tanos pueblos. He was an interesting person, for he learned to speak and write Spanish, denounced his native religion, and operated pack trains, sometimes for the governor, to a place called Los Siete Rios, near present-day Artesia, to trade with Apaches. Yet, he too had become bitter and turned on those for whom he was a favorite.

Like the earlier attempt at rebellion, Esteban Clemente and his followers were discovered. He and his co-conspirators were found guilty of practicing sorcery, communing with the devil, and plotting with Apaches to rebel. Clemente and three other leaders were hanged. Some forty-three others received a public flogging. One of the forty-three flogged was a religious leader from San Juan Pueblo called Popé (also

Popay or Po'pay). Popé resented his treatment and became the organizer of the most successful Indian rebellion in North American history, for the distaste for Spanish rule was not limited to a few southern pueblos. Popé would move to Taos Pueblo, far away from Spanish eyes.

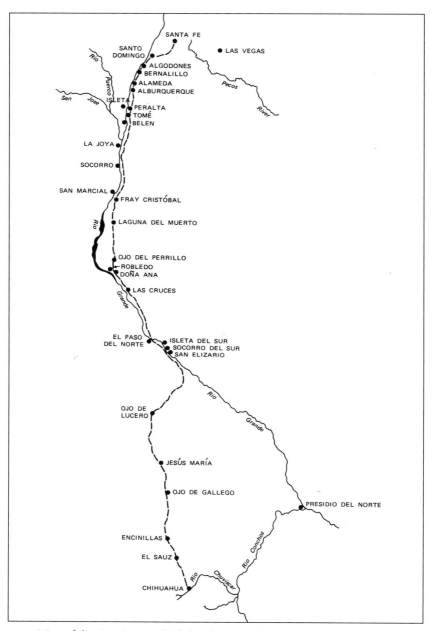

Map of the Camino Real/Chihuahua Trail. From Myra Ellen Jenkins and Albert H. Schroeder, A Brief History of New Mexico *(Albuquerque: University of New Mexico Press, 1974).*

CHAPTER FIVE

Rebellion and Resettlement

✺

On 10 August 1680 the Pueblo Indians of New Mexico united in a coordinated effort to rebel against the Hispanic society. After almost three weeks of violence and death, the Pueblo people, with the help of Apache allies, successfully forced almost all the remaining Spanish settlers out of New Mexico. For the next thirteen years the area of El Paso would be the northernmost Spanish settlement. The Pueblo people had New Mexico to themselves for an interlude that probably turned out differently than expected.

The Pueblo Revolt grew out of the chaos of the Spanish occupation. In addition, it was either a part of, or coincidental with, a greater Indian rebellion that took place throughout the Spanish borderlands, the northern frontier of New Spain. Simply put, the Indians realized that their subjugation to the new society was not worth the benefits that they received in return. Like many other native rebellions, the people felt that a return to traditional ways would result in an improved lifestyle. The method to achieve this goal was to please the deities by ridding themselves of the harbingers of these new, nontraditional lifestyles imposed upon them.

So, a leader known as Popé came to the forefront. A controversial figure to say the least, he claimed to receive communication from

Po-he-yemu, an ancient god, who gave him guidance. Popé was described as a tall and dark person with yellow eyes who worked out of Taos Pueblo and he was able to coordinate the alliance of many of the Pueblo villages in almost total secrecy.

His runners took messages to the individual pueblos, where local leaders organized. Two of his assistants, (Alonso) Catití and (Luís) Tupatú, from Picurís Pueblo, would surface as key players after Popé's death. Eventually, the Pueblo leaders decided upon a day for the rebellion. They sent runners out with knotted cords, each knot representing a day until the planned uprising. But one was captured as rumor spread about the planned insurrection. Governor Antonio de Otermín received the news with skepticism. The idea of a Pueblo rebellion seemed incredulous to him. The Pueblos, he apparently felt, were incapable of coordinating such an event. He would pay for his audacity, for the Pueblos, fearing that he might take action, rebelled early. The resulting violence would strike terror throughout the colony.

North of Santa Fe many of the Hispanic people were caught unaware and killed, sometimes under harrowing circumstances. Those fortunate enough to escape fled to Santa Fe, where, in the fortress that surrounded the main plaza, some one thousand people and over two thousand head of livestock congregated. There the somewhat surprised governor decided to make a stand.

His fortress sat on the north side of the Santa Fe River opposite a series of residences and their church, San Miguel, located south of the river. This neighborhood was the first part of town that was attacked. The reason was quite simple. The first Pueblo Indians to attack Santa Fe came from the southern pueblos, especially those in the Galisteo Basin. Because they came in from the south they encountered a mostly abandoned and completely exposed area.

As Otermín gathered information, took inventory, and organized his defense, he became more convinced that the siege could be lifted. So he ordered a counterattack. He had enough able-bodied men to do serious damage. Perhaps such an example of resolve and fortitude would quell the enthusiasm of the Natives. A daylong battle followed in which the Spanish charged out of the royal fortress. Between two and three hundred Indians were killed before some of the northern Pueblos arrived to divert the Spanish fighters. Despite the heavy losses, the siege continued as the Pueblos cut off the water supply that entered the fortification.

A second foray took place a few days later, on the morning of 20 August, and again the besieged demonstrated their bravery as well as superiority of arms in a furious fight. But the determination of the Pueblo Indians remained intact despite devastating casualties. Governor Otermín remained confident of an ultimate victory, for he felt that the Indians could not sustain the heavy losses inflicted upon them. But with the water supply cut off and more reinforcements arriving from the northern pueblos, the governor's own advisors began to talk of leaving the capital.

Under the circumstances, the governor decided to abandon Santa Fe. But how would this be done? Would they have to fight their way out with women and children in their midst? No matter the scenario, they faced a daunting task.

As they pondered their fate and prepared to act, the people mounting the walls witnessed an odd event. The attackers hanged one of their own from a tree. Apparently the victim was from a southern pueblo and historians can only speculate as to the reason for his execution. Obviously there was disagreement among the Pueblo people. One possible source of conflict was the warning of the pending rebellion, which had leaked from the southern pueblos. Indeed, some Spanish lives were saved because of the warnings. Second, the southerners had taken severe casualties before the northern contingent arrived to join the siege. Quite possibly there was some animosity about the late arrival of the northern allies.

On the morning of 21 August, the front gates were opened and the people inside the fort moved out as orderly and quickly as they could. The men arrayed themselves around the women and children, ready to defend against an attack. But the attack never came. The Pueblo Indians parted ranks and let the hated Spanish leave in peace. Again, theories abound as to why the settlers were allowed to leave. Obviously, the Pueblo Indians already had taken heavy losses, so perhaps they chose not to take more with victory achieved. In the end, common sense prevailed. The colony left after sustaining only five deaths during the siege.

Among their very few possessions that they took south, the settlers carried two statues of Mary. One was an image of María del Sagrario,

La Macana

In a side chapel in the grand old church of San Francisco in Mexico City, sits a small statue of Mary. A label explains that Our Lady of the Aztec War Club or "La Macana" had an incredible history far to the north.

Her real name is Nuestra Señora del Sagrario de Toledo, "Our Lady of the Tabernacle of Toledo." She is a miniature copy of a statue of the same name that resides in Toledo's great cathedral as that city's patronal Madonna. In 1598, Bartolomé Romero took her to New Mexico as a member of Juan de Oñate's first colony. In New Mexico, so the story goes, she was handed down within the family until, in 1674, she was in the possession of Bartolomé's great-granddaughter, who was probably María Romero. At this time, María was a ten-year-old, invalid, and dying girl. She lived with her family in a house located in the neighborhood of Analco in Santa Fe's south side. Bedridden, she had only her statue of María, her namesake, as a companion.

In 1674 a miracle occurred. The statue spoke to María Romero, telling her to rise from the bed and go to the parish church, a remnant of which is the north transept of the current cathedral in Santa Fe. There she was to instruct the priest to convey a message to the people.

The priest, no doubt astounded to see the girl healthy and walking, dutifully followed her instructions. He told the assembled towns-people that the image of Mother Mary had said that if they did not start listening to the priests and living better lives they would be punished severely with a rebellion of the Pueblo Indians.

Word of this miraculous warning spread throughout the young colony and beyond. One missionary, Fray José de Trujillo, working at the Hopi Pueblos, received the story and its warning with glee. He apparently had spent his life seeking martyrdom in the service of his Lord. He relayed the story to his Franciscan superiors in Mexico City, where, a few years later, Fray Agustín de Vetancurt wrote about the prophesy and Fray Trujillo's martyrdom at the Hopi pueblo of Xongopavi during the Pueblo Revolt on 10 August 1680. His book, *Teatro Mexicano*, was published in 1697. Subsequently, Fray Felipe Montalvo included a more complete and exaggerated account of the episode in a book published in 1755. Even Diego de Vargas, governor, leader of New Mexico's resettlement in 1693, and hero of Santa Fe's Fiestas, knew about La Macana.

Many of the Spanish survivors of the Pueblo Revolt took refuge in the royal houses that made up a fortified government structure in

Nuestra Señora del Sagrario de Toledo, La Macana, the statue that miraculously predicted the 1680 Pueblo Indian Revolt to a young girl. From Fray Angélico Chávez, The Lady from Toledo (Fresno, Calif.: Academy Guild Press, 1960). Photograph courtesy Palace of the Governors (MNM/DCA 152683).

Santa Fe. María Romero, by then a young lady, also fled into the fortress, but she left her statue behind.

The Analco neighborhood was the first part of Santa Fe attacked and, during the chaos, the statue was broken. An Indian, probably a former servant, recognized the statue and took her to the fortress, where she was returned to María Romero. So María and her statue of Mary were a part of the exodus south to the El Paso area.

There the local Franciscan priest talked María out of her famous statue. From that moment the statue began a journey south to the Franciscan mission of Tlalnepantla, which is fifteen miles north of Mexico City. The statue stayed there from 1683 until 1754, when she was moved to her semipermanent home at the Franciscan mother church and convent in Mexico City.

While the statue was at Tlalnepantla, someone commissioned a painting depicting the 1680 Pueblo Revolt in New Mexico to serve as a backdrop as well as historical context. The painting included words that described the revolt as well as the miracle associated with the statue. As her story and relationship to the revolt became known, the Mexican Indians, aware that she had a scar on her forehead from a repaired wound, gave her the name of La Macana, which was a Nahuatl-derived name that referred to a war club. They chose that name under the assumption that she had been hit by a *macana* during the Pueblo Revolt. Her iconography has even come to include a small copper macana that she holds in her arms.

La Macana still resides in Mexico City but her painting has been moved and is missing. Yet her miracle and her story is New Mexico's.

Ruts of the Camino Real in the Jornada del Muerto desert,
at Lava Gate. Photograph by Christine Preston in Preston,
The Royal Road: El Camino Real from Mexico City to Santa Fe
(Albuquerque: University of New Mexico Press, 1998).

which was reportedly involved with the miraculous warning of the rebellion. The other was Nuestra Señora del Rosario, La Conquistadora, the very statue that Fray Benavides brought to New Mexico some fifty-five years earlier.

The journey south was harsh and miserable. The people witnessed the revolt's devastation as they came across destroyed homes and churches as well as the lifeless bodies of friends and relatives. Eventually they would learn that some four hundred of their fellow settlers, including twenty-one priests, had died. This did not include those who were missing or who had been accepted within the Pueblo societies.

Death followed them on the trail as well. Some of the wounded and elderly just could not endure the trip. One notable was an elderly matron, doña Ana Robledo, who succumbed on the trail and was buried below the peak just north of Las Cruces that today bears her surname. In fact, it was named for her grandfather Pedro Robledo, who was the first of Oñate's colonists to die on the way north and is buried there as well. The modern county of Doña Ana in southern New Mexico is also a reminder of this woman's last trip.

The exiles also learned that Lieutenant Governor Alonzo García, who had been in the Rio Abajo area when the rebellion broke out, had fled south, apparently abandoning them. Actually, he had waited at Bernalillo and then at Isleta Pueblo, picking up people who were fleeing from the destruction. He had considered marching north but the negative reports that he received from the north convinced him to do otherwise.

Upon hearing that the governor had escaped with a group of people, García headed back north to render assistance and met Otermín as the latter was moving south. After some initial explanations, the governor and García then determined to continue the exodus. They would move the combined colony of twenty-four hundred people south to the area of the mission of El Paso del Norte. They were fortunate to encounter Fray Francisco Ayeta, who was traveling north out of El Paso with a supply train. The timing of their meeting was perfect for the colonists.

The survivors settled along the Rio Grande south of El Paso. The new settlers included a group of natives from Isleta Pueblo, who created a village that has come to be known as Isleta del Sur (Isleta of the South). Meanwhile, Fray Ayeta headed south to argue for resettling New Mexico. His presence began a debate that lasted more than a few years and would not culminate for over a decade.

As people settled into their new villages they continued to debate whether or not to return to the north. Some of the people moved farther south, determined to put New Mexico behind them. All of them grieved.

Two expeditions returned to New Mexico. Governor Otermín led a small force north in late 1681. He went to Isleta and Sandia pueblos and sent out reconnaissance groups to check the other pueblos as far north as Taos and west to the Hopi pueblos. After his patrols returned, the governor determined that his force was too small to stay, so he withdrew, picking up a large contingent of Indians from Isleta, who told him they feared an attack from the northern pueblos. The Tiwa speakers from Isleta were not the only Pueblos in El Paso, for members of the southern Piro pueblos of Alamillo, Senecú, and Socorro also left their homes in the Rio Abajo to move south.

In 1688, Governor Domingo Jironza de Cruzate, serving his second term as leader of the exiled colony, led another small contingent back to the land of the Pueblos. Like Otermín earlier, Jironza found many of the pueblos abandoned for fear of what revenge the Spanish would exact upon them. Perhaps showing inexperience, the governor proved their fear to be justified, for he attacked and burned Zia Pueblo, killing, according to his account, six hundred of its inhabitants.

That same year Diego de Vargas, a lesser nobleman from an established family in Madrid who had a fourteen-year career in Mexico, received the appointment to be governor of New Mexico. He had a clear task: to reestablish the colony in New Mexico. The officials in Mexico City and Madrid had decided not to abandon the troublesome area. Once again the Franciscans helped convince the Spanish government that New Mexico was worthy of settlement.

By 1692, Vargas had organized a force that he thought sufficient to accomplish the task. Many of the men were veterans of Jironza's foray or had survived the rebellion. New recruits joined the ranks to fill out the army.

With a force of fifty soldiers, their officers, ten citizens, one hundred Pueblo Indians, and three Franciscans, Vargas marched north on a historic as well as legendary expedition. He visited all the pueblos, including the new multistoried, double-plaza pueblo that had been converted from the royal fortress in Santa Fe. There, over cups of hot chocolate, he conferred with Luís Picurí, also known as Tupatú, and another leader called Catití:

> I asked him [Luís Picurí] to enter the said tent, where
> affectionate words were showered upon him and
> where he was served chocolate, which he drank with
> the priests, with me, and with others present.

The governor even entered the pueblo and explored the interior.

Vargas, a man around five feet two inches tall who was born with a harelip, learned that Popé had died, probably killed by his own people. More importantly, Vargas believed that the Native leaders had agreed to allow the Spanish colony to return the following year and reoccupy the area. The Pueblo Indians would vacate Santa Fe, allowing Vargas to reclaim it as the capital of New Mexico. Vargas left those meetings pleased that he had accomplished the resettlement of New Mexico without violence of any kind. The difference between his expedition and that of Jironza just four years earlier is striking.

News of Vargas's peaceful accomplishment rapidly spread south. His technique seemed so odd that Carlos Sigüenza y Góngora, one of Mexico's leading intellectuals of the time, published a laudatory account of the "peaceful reconquest" in a short piece that he titled *Mercurio Volante* (The Flying Mercury). Vargas had restored the whole kingdom "without wasting a single ounce of powder or unsheathing a sword." Vargas had become a legend in his day.

So, with great enthusiasm, Vargas returned south to organize the colony for its move back to New Mexico. Many New Mexicans chose to return. Most had been born there and considered the place, however desperate or dangerous it might be, as home. Many of the listed heads of household were women, widowed during the rebellion. As the *mayordomo*, the head of the confraternity, Vargas dedicated the whole expedition to La Conquistadora, or "La Conquista" as he formally called her, and promised to build a proper throne for her veneration. As a result, the governor and the old statue became historically inseparable.

Vargas and his people reached Santa Fe in September and found it still occupied, so they pitched camp on a hillside northwest of town to wait for the Pueblo people to vacate the buildings. But that did not happen. The Spanish endured two blizzards and twenty-two deaths, all the victims less than sixteen years old. As might be imagined, Vargas's captains and soldiers became increasingly impatient.

The waiting period was a strange situation, for Santa Fe was not under siege. Instead, the Pueblo occupants and the Spanish colonists moved freely in each other's respective pueblo and encampment. Over time, however, the sides hardened until it became obvious that the town's fortifications were being improved and the inhabitants had no intention of leaving. Vargas insisted on continued negotiations despite the complaints of his own people.

Finally, in December Vargas consulted with his lieutenants and the clergy and agreed that an attack would need to be initiated. But, he argued, the violence would not start until after Christmas, a holy day of obligation for his Catholic settlement. So, on the snowy 29th of December of 1693, the siege began and Vargas's peaceful reconquest proved illusory.

The resulting battle was fierce and bloody. We can only imagine the contrast of crimson blood on fresh snow. In the end, the Spanish settlers breached the walls of the pueblo and were able to win a complete victory. Vargas took 120 prisoners and ordered Captain Roque Madrid to execute 70 of them outside the fortress, thus trying to set an example just as Oñate had ninety-four years earlier. Madrid fulfilled the orders outside the north wall.

Vargas's decision to resort to violence was not made easily. Once he made the decision, however, he did not lack resolve. He was a man who tried something unheard of during his time, but failed, and after the failure did not hesitate to take the necessary actions for which he was trained.

Partially because of Sigüenza y Góngora's article, the story of Vargas's noble attempt at a peaceful resettlement has persisted throughout the years and is commemorated today during Santa Fe's annual fiestas. The little statue, La Conquistadora, to whom Vargas dedicated the success of his resettlement, plays a major religious role in the fiestas. His promise to her was not fulfilled until 1714, over a decade after his death in 1704, when her throne was created in the north transept of the new parish church dedicated to Saint Francis. Today, the only remnant of that church is her throne, in a much-reduced north transept of St. Francis Cathedral. La Conquistadora still reigns in the temple built by Vargas's followers in fulfillment of his promise.

Vargas's effort in securing New Mexico continued through 1696, three years later, when he pursued and killed Tupatú and the last resisters in the Rio Pueblo Canyon below Picurís Pueblo. Vargas met serious, widespread resistance, ranging from San Ildefonso Pueblo west to Jémez Pueblo as well as north to the pueblos of Taos and Picurís.

The revolt and subsequent Spanish return marked the beginning of a new relationship between the European settlers and the Pueblo Indians. Both Pueblo and Spanish peoples realized that they shared a lot in common, not the least of which were their common nomadic enemies. The abusive practices associated with the encomiendas and zealous, overburdening attempts at conversion changed. A different, more sympathetic type of Franciscan missionary returned to New Mexico. And Spanish soldiers rode next to Pueblo warriors in virtually every subsequent expedition out of New Mexico. One obvious result of the revolt and reconquest was the syncretism of Native and Spanish religions and the preservation of Pueblo traditions as well as land.

This new era brought other changes from life in the previous century. By all indications the Pueblo population stabilized. The decades-long decline stopped. Spanish society began to spread, with new settlements at Santa Cruz in 1695, the establishment of Albuquerque in 1706, and movement up the Chama River to Abiquiu in the middle of the century and, eventually, along the Pecos and Puerco rivers on either side of the Rio Grande Valley. The government established the villages of Truchas and Trampas to serve as buffers against marauding nomadic Plains Indians, also in the middle of the century. Most of the people who volunteered to settle these new places were second- or multi-generation *genízaros*, those descendants of Indians now culturally Hispanic New Mexican. They received land, equipment, and some initial support in exchange for moving to these dangerous places.

The quality of governors appointed to New Mexico was a significant improvement over those of the previous century, and they did not have to contend with the church and state issue because the area was resettled to be maintained as a colony first and missionary field second. The Inquisition was weakened and almost completely disbanded by the end of the century. Though the missionaries successfully argued for the reoccupation of New Mexico to continue the work begun by earlier friars, the Spanish government no longer viewed their work as the overriding justification for reestablishing the burdensome colony. Instead, New Spain wanted New Mexico populated and stable enough to be a defensive buffer, initially against the French and later against the British and their American colonies.

Within a decade of the resettlement, a new, more dangerous enemy appeared in New Mexico. The Comanche Indians acquired the horse

The Rio Puerco

The eighteenth-century expansion of New Mexican society beyond the Rio Grande Valley is well noted in the annals of New Mexico's history. Some villages were settled as defensive buffers, while others were community grants to people seeking opportunity.

The Rio Puerco begins in the Nacimiento Mountains north of Cuba, descends past Cabezón Peak, and empties into the Rio Grande forty-five miles south of Albuquerque. The river no longer flows year-round because intrusive plants have taken over the river bottom, sucking it dry.

The area was never a great attraction for Spanish settlement. The Navajos considered the Rio Puerco part of their territory. Spanish officials had no resources to challenge that claim.

The colonial government commonly granted land in an attempt to pacify an area. Grants in the Rio Puerco could provide a buffer against the Navajo frontier, as well as push it farther from the middle Rio Grande Valley settlements. The first grazing grants for the Rio Puerco were issued in 1753 and 1772. But the two grants, respectively called Nuestra Señora de la Luz and San Fernando y San Blas, did not result in specific settlements.

The subsequent Ojo de Espíritu grant, located by Cabezón Peak, did result in the Rio Puerco's first short-lived settlements. Bernardo Miera y Pacheco's 1779 map of New Mexico documents the villages of Porteria, El Cabezón de los Montoias (Montoyas), and Guadalupe de los Garcias. Consistent Indian raids, exacerbated by a 1774 Navajo uprising, forced the settlers to abandon the area, possibly before Miera y Pacheco finished his map.

Most of the people moved to the Rio Grande villages of Algodones, Bernalillo, and Alburquerque. No one dared to move back to the area until after the Navajos had been pacified and granted a reservation in 1888. Then, it appears, many descendants of the original settlers moved back to reestablish four villages. These villages included San Luís, which was the northernmost settlement, also called La Tijera; Casa Salazar, located on the old site of Porteria; Guadalupe, located on its same location and called Ojo de Padre; and Cabezón, also located on its original site and called La Posta.

The people soon found out that the stories of their elders were true. Life in the Rio Puerco valley was harsh—even without a prevalent danger from Navajo raids. They dug *acequias*, or irrigation ditches, harnessed water behind dikes, reintroduced livestock, and planted staple crops of corn, wheat, and beans. They built adobe houses containing multiperson sleeping quarters, woodstoves, and outhouses. In the warmer months the latter were an attraction for the rattlesnakes that inhabited the area. Even into the middle of the twentieth century, school amounted to a one-room schoolhouse serving all grades. Instead of hostilities, trade and, it appears, some miscegenation took place with the neighboring Navajos.

Probably the inevitable and last decline began with World War I and continued through drought, the Depression, and World War II. The needs of both wars attracted people away from their rural lifestyles. Military service or work beckoned. The Depression, coupled with the activities of state and federal governments, encouraged the remaining few to leave. And, if Albuquerque was not satisfactory, then California seemed opportune.

The federal government helped the process of abandonment when it passed the Taylor Grazing Act in 1934. The government wanted to protect land from overgrazing but, besides strict and sometimes brutal enforcement, it failed to implement a method that would have helped stockowners reduce herds without causing their personal ruin. Then, when the reservoir that provided irrigation water ruptured, both the federal and state governments refused to help the communities fix the breach. Thus the locals could not sustain themselves from either livestock or crops and the area was doomed.

Echoing the earlier activities of the Santa Fe Ring (see chapter 7), the state allowed new owners to fence off parts of the old Ojo del Espíritu grant. This last insult left a legacy of bitterness in the minds of the Rio Puerco inhabitants and their descendents.

Today, all the villages except San Luís are abandoned and in ruins. The villages are melting back into the very terrain from which they were built. The imprints of the old acequias and the fields where plants grew and animals pastured persist. The timeless landscape remains as before.

Yet, there are house trailers and spotty construction, for the families still retain parts of their land. They return and remember. They share and even write about their heritage. Importantly, they are proud and they will not allow their story to die.

and pushed their Apache neighbors south or into the mountains. By 1720, the Jicarilla Apaches, to use one example, were farming in the Cimarron area. Not long thereafter, they moved across the east range into the Dulce area of north-central New Mexico, where their reservation is today.

Whereas Spanish accounts of punitive expeditions before 1700 relate relatively short, successful, and safe episodes, expeditions after that year became longer, less successful, and more dangerous. The enemy that they chased was no longer on foot. They were on horseback and much more formidable.

One exception was the group encountered by the disastrous Pedro de Villasur expedition of 1720. French intruders were rumored to be entering Spanish territory from the north. The viceroy in Mexico City insisted that the governor of New Mexico, Antonio de Valverde, investigate the matter, so Valverde commissioned Villasur, New Mexico's lieutenant governor, to lead an expedition. Villasur and about fifty soldiers, along with some sixty Pueblo Indian auxiliaries, went out on the plains in search of the French.

The New Mexicans traveled to a place that they called "El Cuartelejo." El Cuartelejo, located along the present-day border of Colorado and Kansas, was a group of Pueblo villages established in the 1660s. The Pueblo people, apparently intimidated by Spanish suppression during that time, chose to flee the Rio Grande Valley and place themselves in servitude to the Paduaca Apaches, in whose territory they built their villages. No doubt, more people joined them after the Pueblo Rebellion in 1680 and during the Spanish resettlement in 1692–93. The Spanish made a few attempts to retrieve them but with little success. Instead, El Cuartelejo became a place to rest and trade for Spanish and Pueblo people alike.

Not ironically, a series of small pueblos were established in highly defensive locations in the Dinetah area, where Navajos first lived after migrating to the Southwest. This area is north of present-day Cuba, New Mexico, and encompasses the rugged canyon-cut lands of the Largo and Gobernador rivers. These pueblos, some spectacularly located, are known today as Los Pueblitos, and may have been established for the same reasons as El Cuartelejo. An interesting but unanswered question is how many people from Zia Pueblo and its neighbors moved to these

Detail of Segesser I, an early eighteenth-century hide painting which illustrates Spanish-Indian allies attacking an Apache camp. Original in the collections of the Palace of the Governors. Photograph courtesy Palace of the Governors (MNM/DCA 149798).

new sites in reaction to Jironza's 1688 sacking of that pueblo. The Pueblos preferred to live among their Navajo rivals rather than close to the Spanish. In addition, in about 1700 the Ute Indians acquired the horse and gave more reason for the Pueblo people to fortify themselves.

At El Cuartelejo, both Pueblo and Pauduca Apaches, resident in the area, told Villasur's expedition about white men among their Pawnee enemies. Villasur continued on into present-day Kansas and then north into Nebraska, where, on the morning of 14 August 1720, Pawnee and Oto Indians attacked his encampment. A major battle ensued that lasted more than a few hours. A majority of the Spanish soldiers, including Villasur, were killed. Juan de Archebeque, who was a French merchant taken to translate, and Fray Juan Mingues also died during the battle. At least seventeen survivors lived to tell the tale of the tragedy. All the testimony agreed that the attackers had European or specifically French weapons, but historians are convinced that French soldiers did not participate in the battle. A Spanish diary written by Corporal Felipe de Tamaris, who left it on the battlefield, ended up in the French archives in Canada.

The attackers had rifles but not horses. Because they were on foot, they needed to attack before their enemy could take advantage of the mobility that their horses represented. While the New Mexicans were breaking camp at dawn, they were most vulnerable and indeed suffered a horrible loss that would have repercussions for years to come.

First, let us digress to the story of the Frenchman Archebeque, whose real name was Jean l'Archévèque. Recall that rascal ex-governor Peñalosa who had gone to France at the same time Sieur de La Salle was there. As a result of their arguments to the French king, La Salle was given permission to establish a settlement at the mouth of the Mississippi River.

La Salle's expedition ended in Texas, where Indians and internal fighting doomed all but six of the members. L'Archévèque, a teenager, was one of the survivors found by the Spanish. He was taken to Mexico City, where he testified that he had helped assassinate La Salle. Then he was sent to New Mexico, where he became a merchant and the progenitor of the Hispanic Archebeque family. He joined the ill-fated Villasur expedition as the French translator.

As a result of the battle in Nebraska, the viceroy ordered an inspection of the whole northern frontier of New Spain, from the Gulf of Mexico to Baja California. That report and a subsequent governmental reorganization became the basis of a geographical as well as political reform named "Las Provincias Internas" (The Internal Provinces), in which the northern Spanish border was pulled back to roughly the present international border between the United States and Mexico. The only exception in this reorganization was New Mexico, because, as the reports relate, of the stubbornness of its inhabitants.

Events in Europe certainly affected New Mexico. The formation of Las Provincias Internas, for example, was a part of an overall governmental change called "the Bourbon Reforms." The Bourbon family

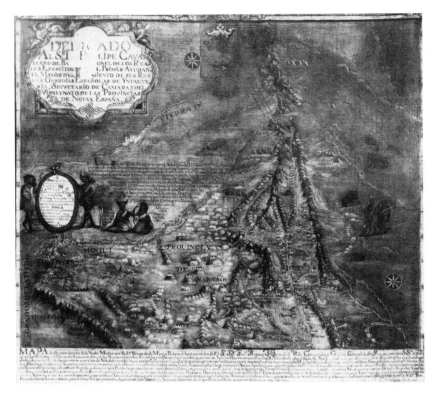

Map of New Mexico, ca. 1760, by Bernardo Miera y Pacheco.
Original in the Fray Angélico Chávez Library. Photograph courtesy
Palace of the Governors (MNM/DCA 135340).

"inherited" the Spanish throne from the Hapsburg dynasty in 1700. This precipitated the War of Spanish Succession, which resulted in a war between France and Spain and explains why the viceroy in Mexico City worried about a French army invading New Mexico. Later in the century, the Bourbons also initiated the governmental reforms mentioned above.

Part of the reforms included the settlement of Alta California in 1767. This gave rise to the possibility of finding a direct overland route between New Mexico and the new west coast settlements.

At the same time, the Catholic hierarchy in Mexico took a renewed interest in the missionary activities in New Mexico. As the Franciscans continued their work, their monopoly was loosened. Three bishops of Durango visited New Mexico, beginning in 1730 with Benito Crespo. Martín de Elizacoechea followed in 1737 and Pedro Tamarón y Romeral traveled through New Mexico in a memorable visitation in 1760. Tamarón was interested in supplanting the Franciscans and possibly establishing diocesan or secular control.

In Santa Fe he noted that Governor Marín del Valle and his wife had paid for the nearly completed military chapel being constructed on Santa Fe's plaza. The new church included a great colored stone-carved stone altar screen, or *reredos*, then being installed behind the altar. Probably carved and painted by Bernardo Miera y Pacheco, the stone relief now graces the huge adobe church of Cristo Rey, which was constructed in the 1930s, in part to house this magnificent work of colonial art. Miera y Pacheco, a native of a small village north of the Spanish city of Burgos, was an artist, cartographer, and political leader. He served as *alcalde* or mayor of Santa Fe and his maps are invaluable treasures. His artwork, which is mostly of religious icons, graces the collections of many current museums. Bishop Tamarón conferred with his vicar, or bishop's assistant, who was appointed vicar of New Mexico in 1730 by Bishop Crespo. This person was the elderly Santiago Roybal, a native-born New Mexican who became New Mexico's first secular priest.

The Franciscans, however, were not ready to relinquish their custody and sent Fray Francisco Atanasio Domínguez north to survey all the churches and write a report of his observations of New Mexico. Father Domínguez accomplished his task in great detail in early 1776. That report has since been translated and published in English. To this day, it is a wonderful source of historical information.

Father Domínguez also teamed up with a local friar, Father Sylvestre Vélez de Escalante, who was stationed at Zuni Pueblo, to lead an expedition up the Chama River Valley and out of New Mexico in an attempt to find a route to California. They took with them the talented Bernardo Miera y Pacheco, whose genius continues to benefit his adopted home of New Mexico to this day. The two Franciscans were aware of Miera y Pacheco's talents and insisted that he be included in the small expedition.

So, in 1776, the priests, Miera y Pacheco, and at least seven other men left Santa Fe and headed northwest into Utah on a six-month journey. They passed the Great Salt Lake and traveled north almost to Utah's

San Rafael by Bernardo Miera y Pacheco. Photograph by Addison Doty. Original in the collections of the Museum of Spanish Colonial Art. From Conexiones: Connections in Spanish Colonial Art, *by Donna Pierce et al. (Santa Fe, NM: Museum of Spanish Colonial Art, 2002). Courtesy Museum of Spanish Colonial Art.*

present northern border. They had hoped to find a large interior river that emptied into the Pacific Ocean on the west coast. Miera y Pacheco even drew this river, named el Rio de Santa Buenaventura, on some of his earlier maps. It is important to remember that such an idea was not too fantastic when we latter-day observers realize that the San Francisco Bay was not discovered until after the first Spanish settlers entered California in 1769. Amazingly, Europeans first discovered it by land. The Spanish were still gathering geographical information. So as not to belittle their efforts or imply ignorance, however, consider that it was Miera y Pacheco who first accurately noted and placed the continental divide. And he did so in a map that dates to about 1760!

Of course, the expedition learned that the river did not exist and they returned south to cross the Grand Canyon close to present-day Page, Arizona. They arrived at the Hopi pueblos, where they received a message left by Fray Francisco Garces. Father Garces had just traveled from the mission of San Xavier del Bac in southern Arizona, then called La Pimería Alta, to southern California and back into the Grand Canyon to the Hopi pueblos. Between the two expeditions the land and distance between Spain's two northernmost colonies were reconnoitered. The journals of both the Domínguez-Escalante and Garces expeditions have been preserved and published in English translation.

∞

Comanche raiding continued to be a serious problem that ebbed and flowed as various governors tried different policies. As part of the Bourbon reforms, New Mexico received a new governor, Juan Bautista de Anza, who took his post in 1779. Anza's eight-year reign arguably was the most successful of all of New Mexico's colonial governors. He brought a wealth of frontier experience with him, for he grew up in the Pimería Alta, where his father of the same name became legendary as the military leader of that harsh area. Anza was instrumental in settling early Alta California. His two most notable achievements in New Mexico were securing peace with the Comanche Indians and raising monetary support for the independence of the United States.

Anza won peace with the Hopi pueblos and then with the Comanches when he led a daring expedition into Colorado to surprise the feared

Comanche leader whom the Spanish called Cuerno Verde. In a battle that raged for almost fifty miles over the plains outside of present-day Pueblo, Colorado, Cuerno Verde and his son were killed, and his band defeated. Anza took the Comanche leader's green horn headdress as a prize and sent it to Mexico along with his report. The eventual fate of that head-piece is a wonderful subject for speculation, for it would be a unique arti-fact today.

Cuerno Verde's defeat impressed the Comanche bands enough for them to meet with Governor Anza at Pecos Pueblo in 1786, where they agreed to peace and to serve as allies as Anza went on to success-fully confront the Apache Indians in southeastern New Mexico. The peace was such that the two societies formed a strong alliance. They began to interact in ways that other people would fail to understand. The interrelations built upon the trade fairs that already existed and two new phenomena unique to New Mexico—the *comancheros* and *ciboleros*—created a special relationship between New Mexicans and the Comanche bands. New Mexican men began to travel out onto the plains to live among the Comanche Indians, where they traded and hunted. For the most part, these men were genízaros who lived in the recently established villages located on the plains' edge. These people, it seems, were comfortable living and operating in two societies. New Mexicans who traded with the Comanches came to be known as comancheros, and those who hunted where known as ciboleros, or buffalo hunters. Obviously, many of the men participated in hunting as well as trading. Comanchero and cibolero activity proved to be a good cementing and lasting bond between the two peoples.

In 1776, thirteen British North American colonies rebelled against their sovereign. Spain immediately supported the colonies with covert aid and on 14 June 1779, declared war on Great Britain. Governor Anza, like all Spanish officials, received notice of the declaration of war and was requested to collect a tax of 2 pesos (about $60 in today's equivalencies) for each full-blooded Spanish subject and 1 peso for each mixed-blood or Native subject. Anza asked to exempt the Hopi and Zuni pueblos because of the state of their poverty. Anza was able to send 3,677 pesos from his poor, currency-scarce province. Arizona, California, Texas, as well as all the other Spanish colonies throughout the world, sent money to help Spain in the war against Great Britain.

María Rosa Villalpando

Josiah Gregg, in his ever-popular 1844 publication, *Commerce of the Prairies*, gave an account of an old lady, recently passed away, who had become legendary in St. Louis. While Gregg recounted the legend, the lady was real and the story is based in fact. The ancient lady was born in New Mexico and lived an astounding life.

The woman, whom Gregg identified merely as a daughter of "a Spaniard named Pando," was in reality María Rosa Villalpando, from the Taos Valley. Her story began in 1760 when she was living in the family hacienda at Ranchos de Taos with her husband and son. Her son's name was Joseph Julian Jaques.

On 14 August 1760 a band of Comanche Indians raided the hacienda. When the fighting ended all fourteen men in the compound were killed and some fifty-five women and children, including María Rosa, were taken captive. While many of the captives were later returned, María Rosa would not be one of the lucky.

The Comanches traded her to the Pawnees, with whom she lived for ten years. Sometime during her first six years in captivity she had a son, who stayed with her and was named Antoine Xavier. In 1767, she met a young French trader named Jean Sale dit Lajoie, who fathered her third child, named Lambert. Three years later Sale dit Lajoie ransomed her and took her to the new village of St. Louis.

There she became known as Marie Rose and on 3 July 1770, she married Jean Sale. Three more children were born to the couple but only one, Helene, survived childhood.

After twenty-two years of marriage Jean Sale decided to go to

In the end, we all know that the colonies succeeded in their quest, but few realize the key role of Spain, much less New Mexico's small part.

World events continued to impact New Mexico. Certainly Spain's expansion to, and trade in, the Philippine Islands (named for King Felipe II, the same king who gave Oñate permission to settle New Mexico) also gave rise to the famous Manila Galleon, or East Indies trade, the route of which included transcontinental shipments across Mexico. Some of the goods that originated in China and the South

France and take Lambert with him. After two years in Europe, Lambert returned without his father. From then on Marie Rose was known as the widow Sale, hinting that Jean Sale may have died in France.

In 1802, María Rosa's New Mexico son, Joseph Julian, crossed the plains in search of his mother. How he learned that she had survived and was living in St. Louis is not documented but easy enough to surmise. Her story, shared by herself, had made it across the plains. Joseph Julian could only conclude that the widow Sale, known as Marie Rose, and with some ancestral name sounding like "Pando," was his mother. Why else risk the daunting trip nineteen years before the opening of the Santa Fe Trail?

María Rosa did not hesitate to acknowledge her first son and immediately introduced him to his half brothers and half sister. They amicably made a legal agreement in which Joseph Julian gave up any claim to his mother's St. Louis estate in favor of his half–sister, Helene. In exchange, he received two hundred pesos, a lot of money at that time, and returned to New Mexico.

María Rosa died in St. Louis on 27 July 1830, almost seventy years after she was taken captive in New Mexico. Her son's descendants still live in northern New Mexico and her daughter's descendants have their home in St. Louis. One of her St. Louis grandsons, Antoine Leroux, had moved to Taos by 1824, where, in 1833, he married into the New Mexican Vigil family.

Today, the Taos Valley communities of Talpa and Cañon include many Jaques-, Villalpando-, and Leroux-surnamed people, who are distant cousins. The history of María Rosa Villalpando, in fact, is far more colorful and influential than the legend.

Pacific came to New Mexico. For example, Chinese pottery, porcelain, the famous Spanish shawls or *mantones*, and the large tortoiseshell head ornaments or combs worn by women, called *peinetas*, became fairly common in New Mexico. In fact, trade was so extensive that evidence exists that New Mexican colonial governors ate oysters on the half shell in Santa Fe!

However, the young United States would prove to be more aggressive than Great Britain or France. As has been seen, Frenchmen had traveled to New Mexico since the seventeenth century. Now the French and Indian War and then the American Revolution had changed the dynamics of North America. For now France had lost its possessions in North America. Many of the French Americans, especially in the Mississippi and Ohio river valleys, chose to become subjects of Catholic Spain. Frenchmen like Pedro de Vial out of New Orleans, or, even earlier, the Mallet Brothers out of what was called the Illinois country, traveled great distances, crossing the plains between what became Spanish New Orleans and St. Louis to New Mexico. Not surprisingly, New Mexicans continued their own exploratory travels. One soldier, Juan Lucero, made no less than thirteen known journeys out onto the plains at the end of the eighteenth and into the nineteenth century.

Then European events changed the dynamics again. France, under Napoleon Bonaparte, pressured Spain for the cession of Louisiana in 1799, turned around and sold it to the United States in 1803, and then invaded Spain and deported the king. Napoleon placed his brother Joseph on the throne as the king of Spain. The Spanish never quit resisting and referred to this new king as "Pepe Botella," in reference to his drinking problem.

Of course, Thomas Jefferson, the president of the United States, needed a detailed description of the newly acquired territory's boundaries. A series of official and semi-official expeditions took place. For New Mexico the two most noteworthy of these expeditions were the Meriwether Lewis and William Clark expedition and a lesser, but important, journey led by Zebulon Montgomery Pike.

Pike, an army officer, was sent to find the official boundary between the United States and Mexico. Instead, he entered New Mexican or Spanish territory and was arrested in the present-day San Luis Valley in southern Colorado. He was initially taken to Santa Fe, where he was put under house arrest. Santa Fe did not impress him, as he rather offhandedly described the old capital as having

> the same effect as a fleet of the flat bottomed boats, which are seen in the spring and fall seasons descending the Ohio River. There are two churches, the magnificence of whose steeples form a striking contrast to the miserable appearance of the houses.

The New Mexican government next transported him to Mexico City. Pike apparently had a very good memory, for he kept a diary of his trip and though the Mexican authorities took it from him, he was able to recompile it from memory and he published it as a book after his return to the United States. Many years later, in the twentieth century, Pike's original diary was located in the Mexican archives and found to be almost identical to his publication.

Lewis and Clark did not enter New Mexican territory, for they traveled farther north on a mission to cross the continent in search of a good transcontinental trade route. But their presence was known and Juan Lucero was dispatched to encounter them. He did not find them, but the viceroy correctly saw all this interest in the west as a harbinger to eventual United States expansion.

New Spain, or Mexico, had other priorities. Mexico and all the other Spanish colonies were moving toward independence. The example set by the United States, Spanish policy, European Enlightenment philosophy, and regional pride all contributed to the process. Furthermore, how could the Spanish colonists remain loyal to a French pretender sitting on a Spanish throne? Pepe Botella was a perfect excuse to sever relations.

As a result, the exiled Spanish government invited representatives from throughout the empire to Spain. New Mexico, for the only time in its history, sent an official representative to participate in the Spanish government. The representative took a seat in the *Cortes*, which was meeting in the port city of Cádiz, Spain's southwestern-most city.

New Mexico selected don Pedro Pino, a successful landowner from a prominent local family. Pino left New Mexico in 1812 and traveled to Spain. In the port city of Cádiz he presented a report on conditions in New Mexico in which he stressed New Mexico's poverty and exposure to foreign elements:

> The purchase of Louisiana by the United States has
> opened the way for the Americans to arm and incite
> the wild Indians against us; also the way is open for the
> Americans to invade the province. Once this territory
> is lost, it will be impossible to recover.

Given the reality of the situation, the exiled Spanish government could do nothing and Pedro Pino received nothing for his efforts. During his return trip he acquired a fancy carriage in Mexico. It became the talk of New Mexico. New Mexicans summed up his trip with the now famous refrain,

> *Don Pedro Pino se fue*
> *Don Pedro Pino vino*

or,
don Pedro Pino went,
don Pedro Pino came.

Although the exiled Spanish government regained control of Spain from France, the damage had been done and the independence movement successfully advanced throughout Spanish America. Mexico, under the unfurled banner with the image of Guadalupe, began the struggle that won its independence on 16 September 1821. New Mexico, which did not directly participate in the movement, only received reports of what was happening. Upon receiving word of independence, the last of sixty-eight Spanish governors had a tricky problem with which to contend and, as we shall see, he solved that problem in true New Mexican fashion.

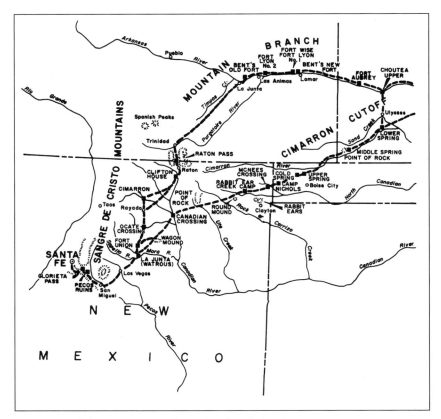

Map of the Santa Fe Trail. National Park Service.
From Myra Ellen Jenkins and Albert H. Schroeder,
A Brief History of New Mexico *(Albuquerque:*
University of New Mexico Press, 1974).

CHAPTER SIX

The Day of the Wedding

Mexican Independence
and the Beginning
of a New Identity

&Ͽ;

In July of 1821, New Mexico's last Spanish governor, Fecundo Melgares, received word that New Mexico was now a part of the newly independent country of Mexico. Melgares immediately decided to share the information with his assembled constituency in Santa Fe's plaza, where he announced a celebration for the occasion. Beginning with a High Mass at the *parroquia*, the celebration continued through the night to the next day. Melgares knew his people well, for he was accepted as New Mexico's first Mexican governor. He formally swore allegiance to the new government in September.

In the time leading up to independence, although foreigners, both French and from the United States, continued to trickle into the province, life had not changed much. Society was still rural. Very few settlements existed and they were generally distant from each other. Sheep had become the main livestock. Navajos, Utes, and Apaches continued to raid both Hispanic and Pueblo settlements; infant mortality was high; seasonal life patterns worked together with religious requirements. Some new Hispanic families, even a few people direct from Spain, moved into New Mexico to intermarry and supplement the older families. The Sosayas, some new Ortizes, and Miera y Pacheco are a few examples of family names that came to New Mexico during the eighteenth century. Even in the eighteenth century and into the Mexican period natives of Spain such as Damaso López, Manuel Alvarez, and, later, Father Damaso Taladrid moved to New Mexico.

Society had grown and spread by the time of Mexican independence, but the number of priests serving the area had dwindled. The fortress that contained the government buildings had also shrunk. Renovated at the end of the eighteenth century, by 1821 it was dilapidated. The old *presidio real* now became *El Palacio del Gobierno*, "the government palace," which would be mistranslated "The Palace of the Governors."

While lifestyles changed slowly, Mexican independence would bring change even more profound than the Pueblo Revolt and almost as shocking as the arrival of Europeans. The next twenty-five to twenty-six years, a very short time relatively speaking, would be crucial in the history of New Mexico. If likened to a marriage with a courtship, then the Mexican period was the day of the wedding. And it was a shotgun wedding, for the period ended with the Mexican War, the result of which would weld Hispanic, Native American, and United States societies together into the present.

Continuing the analogy, all that preceded the Mexican period set the stage for this eventual union. And, like old-fashioned weddings, things tended to get more hectic as the principles moved closer to the assigned date. The day of the wedding is chaotic, if not panicky, as things happen quickly.

So too did New Mexico's move through the Mexican period. Mexico, like the United States, no longer existed as a colonial member of a larger mercantile system. Now it could do business with any other country. Its borders were open for business.

Just over eight hundred miles across relatively flat land already explored and well known, the young United States, not even fifty years old itself, would become an important trading partner with Mexico via the Santa Fe Trail. The trail would extend from Missouri, which became a state in 1824, to New Mexico. At Santa Fe the Santa Fe Trail connected with the old Camino Real, the Royal Road that extended into Mexico proper. The two trails effectively connected the western frontier of the United States with north-central Mexico.

On 13 November 1821, Captain Pedro Ignacio Gallego, leading a contingent of over four hundred men, rode out of Puertocito de la Piedra Lumbre pass, just west of present-day Las Vegas, New Mexico. They saw, coming off the plains, a travel-worn group of six foreigners led by William Becknell, who had crossed the plains from St. Louis. They may not have known that just a few months earlier, Fecundo Melgares, New Mexico's governor, had sworn allegiance to the new government in Mexico. The two contingents of men cautiously closed on each other, curious but leery. The Americans were surprised to see the Mexicans making signs of friendship and welcome. They were more relieved to hear through the difficulties of translation that they would be escorted on to Santa Fe, where, on 15 November 1821, the governor fondly welcomed them. As a result, Becknell has forever received credit for "opening" the Santa Fe Trail.

The trail extended out of northern New Mexico onto the plains to take various routes to the Arkansas River and across Kansas to Missouri. Over the years, the trail's eastern terminus moved west, beginning at St. Louis, then moving to Westport, then to Council Grove. The Missouri, Mississippi, and Ohio rivers effectively connected the Santa Fe Trail to the eastern seaboard. New Mexican merchants like Manuel Alvarez and Manuel Armijo, a governor on three different occasions during this period, kept bank accounts in New York. Alvarez had agents and accounts in London as well. The Santa Fe Trail truly welded New Mexico to the United States, for not only was it financially beneficial to both sides, but the social and cultural connections probably were even more influential.

The Santa Fe Trail would become a commercial route over which mules and hard specie (silver and gold) went to the United States in exchange for utilitarian goods like cloth, tools, needles, and even thread. Caravans at times returned from Mexico with over $200,000 in gold or silver. By the 1830s over half the commerce on the trail extended into Mexico proper and the silver peso became the main medium of exchange in Missouri. The peso helped to stabilize the monetary system of all of the western states. By the end of the Mexican period, at least half of the trade was owned and operated by Mexican citizens. Many United States merchants took Mexican wives and converted to Catholicism, thus avoiding Mexican import taxes. New Mexico, at the crucible of this international trade, would be changed forever.

∞

Simultaneously, a fad in hats began in Europe and spread to the United States, giving rise to the beaver felt industry. This industry peaked just as Mexico gained its independence. Beaver trappers, working for large companies, permeated the Rocky Mountain West, some traveling as far as California seeking beaver skins, from which the felt was made for the popular "top hats" then in fashion.

The trappers went into the mountains, where they worked in brigades, large groups, through the winter to get the pelts at their best. At the end of the season, all the trappers met in rendezvous at designated places to turn over their catches for money from the company. The company then transshipped the accumulated furs downriver (the Platte and Missouri rivers) to St. Louis for distribution.

The rendezvous system, as it was called, benefited New Mexico. Rather than stay in the mountains, the trappers could take their goods to New Mexico, in the southern Rockies, where the pelts could be shipped to St. Louis on the Santa Fe Trail. They could also spend the summer in northern New Mexico, which seemed preferable to never leaving the mountains.

There were some drawbacks for the mountain men in New Mexico. Mexican officials expected trappers to pay for a license to trap in Mexican territory. Mexico was going through its own growing pains as a young country and the foreigners would be affected. A new liberal constitution was established in 1824, but its eventual erosion would lead to a series of rebellions across the north that included New Mexico and would result in Texas's independence in 1836.

∞

Mexican President Antonio López de Santa Anna appointed his own man to be governor of New Mexico. Governor Albino Pérez had a mission to assure that the new policies of governmental centralization and taxation would be carried out. The policies, as well as Governor Pérez, quickly upset the local population enough to where a rebellion occurred in 1837. Pérez was overthrown and killed. The rebellion turned out to be a local manifestation of a larger revolt against Santa Anna throughout northern Mexico.

Manuel Armijo, who had been New Mexico's governor earlier and whose lineage came from prominent Rio Abajo families, gathered a militia to defeat the rebels, thus establishing himself as a local hero in the eyes of the national government. Ironically, Armijo fulfilled a major goal of the revolt, for he was officially appointed governor, thus putting a local and not an outsider in office.

In 1841, shortly after its independence, Texas made an attempt to claim New Mexico and sent an expedition out of Austin that was mis-led by a New Mexican scout from Taos, attacked by Comanche Indians, and left on foot near the Wichita Mountains in Oklahoma. The nearly starved and broken-up expedition was rescued in various stages by New Mexican shepherds and then arrested by Governor Armijo, who used the opportunity to claim yet another military victory and so enhance his reputation in distant Mexico City. The Mexican government ordered that the Texans be marched south to Mexico City, where those who survived were eventually released.

The United States consul, Manuel Alvarez, survived an attempted assassination as a result of the 1841 Texan attempt to claim New Mexico. When Governor Armijo left town on his best mule and in a powder-blue uniform to review the Texan prisoners at Anton Chico, his nephew and others broke into the consul's store and attacked him. They believed that he had assisted the Texans. After sustaining a knife wound on his face, Alvarez was saved when Guadalupe Miranda, the secretary of the government, interceded and stopped the attack. Later, in a fit of bravado, Alvarez claimed that he was "about to master" his attackers when Miranda showed up.

Governor Armijo returned to Santa Fe from his "victory" over the

Governor Manuel Armijo, ca. 1845. Original drawing in the collections of the Palace of the Governors. Photograph courtesy Palace of the Governors (MNM/DCA 50809).

Texans (as he would have everyone believe) at Anton Chico to hear about the attack on Alvarez. He eventually allowed the consul to leave for the United States where he unsuccessfully petitioned Secretary of State Daniel Webster for reparations for himself and other United States citizens who had been adversely affected. Some of the claimed injuries dated back to the 1837 rebellion when Armijo returned to power. The United States merchants actually had supported Armijo with monetary contributions.

But Texans still sought to divert the trade on the Santa Fe Trail to themselves. Or, did they now seek revenge for the Mexican handling of their mismanaged expedition? Officially sanctioned groups of Texans began to wait at the Arkansas River to attack unsuspecting Mexican caravans.

The problem with that strategy was the reality that merchants from both Mexico and the United States had become partners and pooled their resources. Thus, no such target—a purely Mexican caravan— existed. In fact, the American merchants found the "pirates of the lone star" so frustrating that they succeeded in convincing the U.S. government to provide military escorts to the Arkansas River. At one point the U.S. Army, with official approval, crossed the Arkansas River to arrest a band of Texans in Mexican territory. Another group of Texans was arrested for the attack and murder of some Mexican merchants. (One of the victims was a Chaves, and the site of the outrage was named for him but has become "Jarvis" instead of "Chaves" Creek in Kansas.) Some of the perpetrators were tried and hanged in Missouri. Nonetheless, some Texans did succeed in raiding the new settlement of Mora, located in a valley called Lo de Mora, ("place of the blackberry or mulberry"), nestled on the eastern slope of the Sangre de Cristo Mountains.

Governor Armijo occasionally received reports of Texan "raiders" on the prowl. This information originated from Cheyenne Indians, who reported to Bent's Fort, located on the Arkansas River. The proprietors, Charles and William Bent, along with former trapper Ceran St. Vrain, made sure that word got to the governor.

On one occasion, in 1843, the warning system backfired. Armijo decided to send a contingent out to escort an incoming caravan. Captain Ventura Lobato led a group of New Mexicans, most of whom were from Taos Pueblo. While going through the mountains toward present-day Cimarron, a group of Texans ambushed them, inflicting heavy casualties on the New Mexicans. Most of the men who died were from Taos Pueblo. As a result of this ambush, Armijo closed the border to all trade.

The effects of Texas's early activities and aspirations in New Mexico would play out for many years in tragic attempts at revenge during the Mexican War, continue through the Civil War as contested in New Mexico, and persist until today, where parts of New Mexico still harbor anti-Texan feelings the reasons for which are lost in time.

∞

An immediate result of the 1841 Texan expedition to New Mexico was a public reaction against those perceived to be in alliance with the invaders. Naturally, many of the local population condemned the merchants and traders from the United States. Some of the latter were threatened and even attacked. Two of these people decided to leave New Mexico, and invited friends and family to join them in a journey over the "Old Spanish Trail" to southern California. William Workman and John Rowland successfully led their band of exiles, a group of twenty-three Anglos and three Mexicans, to San Gabriel, California, to become settlers initially in a place called La Puente, now a suburb of Los Angeles. Their journey is noteworthy for a couple of reasons.

The trail over which they traveled opened as early as 1827, allegedly by Antonio Armijo, a New Mexican following a long tradition of looking for a more direct route to California. Armed with the knowledge gleaned from earlier expeditions, such as that led by Domínguez and Escalante, Armijo's idea and even his route were not new. A southern route through Sonora already had been heavily traveled, serving as the primary feeder to the west coast colony. Armijo followed known trails up the Chama River Valley from Abiquiu, through the Four Corners area, and into Utah, thus avoiding the Grand Canyon by going north of it. He then headed southwest into the desert, where he is credited with encountering a natural spring at a place that would become the world-famous gambling capital, Las Vegas, Nevada. From there, he crossed the Colorado River and made the perilous journey across the Mojave Desert. He entered the Los

Angeles basin through El Cajon Pass, which cuts through the San Gabriel Mountains near present-day San Bernardino.

Originally, the trail was sparsely traveled, as it was at the time of the Workman and Rowland trip. But with the discovery of gold at Sutter's Mill in California in 1849, the trail became an important commercial route over which New Mexican sheep were taken to feed California's increasing population. Among other influences, place names like Chávez Ravine, the partial present site of Dodger Stadium in Los Angeles, are vestiges of New Mexico's nineteenth-century connection to California via the Old Spanish Trail. The ravine is named for a shepherd from New Mexico who kept his flock there waiting for sale.

Another person worthy of note is Albert Toomes, who joined the Workman and Rowland party to travel to California. Earlier that year of 1841, Toomes was in St. Louis. He wanted to go to California and had just missed joining a major caravan that recently embarked. That caravan would travel over the newly opened northern route to the west coast, through the "South Pass" at the continental divide in Wyoming. That caravan became known as the Bartleson-Bidwell wagon train and went down in history as the first immigrant caravan to complete the trip over the Oregon Trail to California. Toomes missed them by seven days. So he decided to travel down the more familiar Santa Fe Trail to New Mexico, where he arrived in Santa Fe within days of the announced departure of the Rowland and Workman group. He rushed to Abiquiu to join them and subsequently completed his trip to California, arriving in December of 1841. There he heard that the caravan that he missed in Missouri had arrived. That earlier, more historically known expedition arrived in northern California only a week before the New Mexicans.

∞

All of this intrigue, trade, violence, and travel hints of change that was occurring much more rapidly than heretofore. To be sure, the birth of two nations, Mexico and the United States, within the same hemisphere, would result in change. Mexican governmental policy, such as opening its borders to international trade, directly affected New Mexico. Other policies relative to land, the church, and even national chauvinism also affected New Mexico.

Most of New Mexico's land grants actually originated during the Mexican period. Many of the grants issued under Spanish administrations occurred toward the end of the colonial period, or immediately preceding the Mexican period. Manuel Armijo gained some notoriety for his generosity, not only for the amount of land he doled out but because he granted land to the *americanos* as well as his own people. Over time some of these grants became exaggerated in their size or lost, not in memory, but for lack of paper documentation, which led to legal shenanigans.

Most individuals received grants, called *suertes* (literally "lucks") through the luck of the draw. People received these grants through a common petition to create a new community or village. A group of people would petition the governor for permission to settle an area along a river. For a defined distance the river bottom would be divided into equal parts and numbered. One part was left for the church, official buildings, and the town square or plaza. Each portion had river frontage. Then individual petitioners drew a number, many times notched on a stick. The corresponding lot was theirs. Thus the individual received property through the luck, or suerte, of the draw.

Work of settlement began once the property was defined. Everyone helped to dig the *acequias*, or irrigation ditches. Usually they helped each other build their houses, which were built above the irrigated fields and next to the main ditch, called the *acequia madre*. The mother ditch ran down each side of the river and fed all the smaller ditches, called *venas* ("veins"). All the land above the bottomlands was specifically defined, in many cases by physical landmarks. This land was held in common for pasturage.

The Native American, Spanish, and then Mexican systems did not have the Anglo American idea of owning property in fee simple, which meant that the land was yours to use or not to use. Rather, landownership was under a system of usufruct, which meant it belonged to the owner as long as he or she used it. Otherwise it reverted to the community or the government. This simple difference in ownership would become a legal focal point for legitimizing or disapproving Spanish and Mexican land grants after New Mexico became a part of the United States.

As populations expanded and people built churches in their humble villages, the Catholic Church underwent change as well. The Franciscans had gone years without real replenishment so an already scarce group had become even more undermanned. Then the Mexican government decided to require all Iberian-born Spaniards to either take an oath of loyalty to the new government or leave the country. Under this policy only one Franciscan was allowed to stay in New Mexico. He could remain because of his advanced age and he lasted until his death in 1841.

Supplying New Mexico as well as the rest of the country with native-born secular clergy became a national priority for Mexico. New Mexicans such as Father Juan Felipe Ortiz from Santa Fe became leaders in the New Mexican church. Padre Ortiz received the appointment of vicar forane from José Antonio Luareano de Zubiría y Escalante, the bishop of Durango. The vicar's first cousin, Ramon Ortiz, became the pastor in El Paso. Padre Antonio José Martínez from Taos emphasized education and helped bring the first printing press to New Mexico. José Manuel Gallegos, born in Abiquiu, established himself as a vibrant community leader in Albuquerque's San Felipe de Neri parish. These and many others received their ecclesiastical education in Durango, Mexico, where they were taught theology and church law as well as patriotic fervor for their new country. Padre Martínez encouraged and even arranged for the initial educational preparation for subsequent priests from New Mexico. These priests also went to Mexico for their education and ordination before returning north. Padre Martínez's school in Taos is the most obvious example of this. Also notable is Padre Martínez's openness, for he admitted young ladies to his school.

Still, the number of clergy, although overwhelmingly native New Mexicans, never fulfilled New Mexico's needs. As a result, a lay organization became prominent as it filled a religious as well as social vacuum. The Hermandad de Nuestro Padre Jesús Nazareno, or the Hermanos Penitentes, became a prominent and influential organization at this time. In many ways they have remained so up to the present.

These very religious people, drawn closer to their God by their desperate circumstances and essentially rural lifestyles, turned to themselves and a God who seemed to them very close and personal. As Fray Angélico Chávez noted in his booklength essay on New Mexico, these people lived under the same circumstances and at the same latitude as

Padre Antonio José Martínez, ca. 1848. Original daguerreotype in the collections of the Albuquerque Museum. Photograph courtesy Palace of the Governors (MNM/DCA 11262) and the Albuquerque Museum (PC 1998.27.29).

those in southern Spain and the Middle East. Their celestial point of view was pretty much the same. So these people organized, selected their own leaders, built their own places of worship so they would not conflict with the church, and developed their own rituals, most significantly around Easter week.

Their *moradas*, or places of worship, were often constructed outside of the community. These single-storied, usually L-shaped, almost windowless, and mud-floored buildings became community centers away from the community. The *cofradias*, or brotherhoods, practiced their religion, always considered Catholic, and relived the Passion of Christ during Easter week, to the point of symbolically crucifying someone to a cross. The person was tied (rather than nailed) to the cross and the rituals included an uphill procession to a calvary or small hill a short distance from the morada.

As non-Catholics moved into New Mexico during the Mexican period as well as after, the Penitentes became more and more secretive. These new people, it seems, saw the Penitentes and their manifestation of faith as an oddity. Eventually, as will be seen, the Catholic Church itself condemned these people. And that has left a rift in the community that lingers into the present.

There has been some debate among historians about the origins of the Penitentes in New Mexico. Some argue that the Penitentes came to New Mexico with the very first Spanish settlers. They can point to the existence of such organizations in Spain as well as to the fact that many of Oñate's group, including the governor himself, practiced a severe form of penance, including self-flagellation. There is no evidence, however, that they practiced in any kind of organized group setting. Oñate, for example, went off by himself to administer his self-imposed penance.

Certainly, as well, confraternities or brotherhoods existed in New Mexico from the first settlement. The confraternity devoted to La Conquistadora was practicing as early as 1631. This society led prayer sessions as well as processions, but again, there is no evidence of the types of worship generally associated with the latter-day Penitente organizations. This is true, as well, of the more recent organization formed to support Our Lady of Light, associated with Santa Fe's Castrense Chapel in 1761.

Another explanation for the origins of the Penitentes is that they grew out of the lay organization called the Third Order of St. Francis. These people took more stringent vows of obedience and faith, and supported the Franciscans in their work. Some historians have surmised the members of this order moved to fill a religious void when the Franciscans were replaced.

Suffice it to say that all these Penitente organizations developed in a very Hispanic context, and it and they evolved in environments distant from the homeland. The official names of New Mexico's Penitente groups remain exactly the same as those found in Spain today. A comparison of their respective regulations for membership also shows them to match very closely. We thus need to consider latter-day influences from Spain and Mexico, for both areas shared forms of this phenomenon. Did a traveler direct from Seville, for example, share nineteenth-century Penitente practices with New Mexicans? Or, more likely, did such practices, like so many cultural influences, travel directly from Spain to Mexico, where, eventually, in some form it traveled to the north?

Probably, all of the above antecedents came together with a lack of clergy to create a sudden escalation of the Penitente movement during the Mexican period. This movement would receive added incentive as a religious as well as cultural and political reaction to a mostly Protestant influx of people after the Mexican period.

Nevertheless, the Catholic Church in New Mexico continued under the able leadership of the vicar, Juan Felipe Ortiz.. Ortiz led his local church during difficult times. The bishop, himself aghast at the practices of the Penitentes, made the arduous journey north from Durango on three different occasions, in 1833, 1845, and 1850. Despite the dearth of priests along with an unfavorable political environment in Mexico, the Mexican church took an interest in New Mexico.

∞

More change loomed on the horizon. Certainly the many newcomers visiting and moving into the area brought with them their cultural baggage. This ranged from language to religion. The newcomers' aggressive business tactics did not go unnoticed; rather, some New Mexicans, themselves, learned to practice the same techniques and even take advantage of the *extranjeros*, or foreigners. Gambling halls, owned by locals and, in one noteworthy case, by a woman, catered to the foreigners. These sons of the "Puritan Ethic" encountered customs in New Mexico that they found difficult to accept.

Women, for example, had rights of inheritance and possession of property in New Mexico. The laws provided protection from spousal abuse to a far greater extent than in the United States. A woman in New Mexico could initiate legal proceedings against men, including her husband. Some of these cultural differences may explain why Gertrudis Barceló, known then and now as "Doña Tules" or "Trudy," for Gertrude, received such an unfair reaction from American writers.

Doña Tules came to be famous because she became fairly wealthy running a successful bar and gambling den in Santa Fe. It appears that her customers from the United States, unlike the locals who frequented her establishment, could not accept the fact that a woman could run a business that, more times than not, divested them of their money. No woman would have had such an opportunity in the United States at that time.

Priests frequenting saloons and hugging friends and family in public view also struck the extranjeros as lacking morality. Most of those clergy were natives of New Mexico, so they had a familiarity with their flocks born out of decades of sharing a community with them. Father Martínez of Taos became an unfair recipient of criticism. Among many things, he was condemned for having children and, therefore, direct descendants. His work in education, printing and publishing, and leadership in politics were overlooked.

∞

America's undeniable march toward New Mexico did not take New Mexicans by surprise. James K. Polk, elected president of the United States in 1843, campaigned on the stated ideal of Manifest Destiny. The United States, he claimed, had a God-given right or destiny to become a transcontinental nation. Fulfilling that destiny would be his priority if elected.

The concept of Manifest Destiny was not new or unknown either in the United States or in other nations. For example, Spain and Mexico

Commercial Agency Seal for Santa Fe, Mexico, 1843.
Original in the collections of the Palace of the Governors.
Photograph courtesy Palace of the Governors (MNM/DCA 146019).

had a historic understanding of the United States' ambitions. As early as 1783 the Spanish ambassador to France wrote to his king that the United States, "born a pigmy" with the help of Spain and France,

> will grow up, become a giant and be greatly feared in the Americas. Then it will forget the benefits that it has received . . . and only think in its own aggrandizement.

United States recognition of Texas as a sovereign nation while Mexico officially considered it a department in rebellion, plus Texas's exaggerated border claims and subsequent conflicts with New Mexico, clearly indicated the great possibility of change in New Mexico. Even American merchants living in New Mexico openly stated the obvious. Upon receiving news of Polk's election, Charles Bent in Taos wrote that he was "fearful that this election will cause difficulty between this [Mexico] and our country." Obviously, as well, Governor Armijo's 1843 closure of New Mexico's ports of entry was an attempt to limit foreign influence.

War was declared when Mexico refused to sell its northern half to the United States' ambitious president. Only a few congressmen opposed the declaration of war. One of these men openly challenged the president's reasons for war. That man was Abraham Lincoln, then a freshman congressman from Illinois.

Secretary of State James Buchanan sent out a confidential circular, a copy of which Manuel Alvarez in Santa Fe received, in which he illogically wrote,

> We go to war with Mexico solely for the purpose of conquering Honorable peace.

President Polk and Congress thought that the conflict would end quickly. Instead, the war lasted two years and became the United States' first unpopular war. The press referred to the war as Mr. Polk's war.

Word of war reached New Mexico on 17 June 1846. Once again Armijo closed the borders. This time his action proved unnecessary, since all Santa Fe Trail caravans bound for New Mexico had been stopped at the United States end of the trail. Only the army led by Brigadier General Stephen Watts Kearny was allowed through. The Army of the West was made up of soldiers from Missouri and Ohio as well as other western states and locales, including a company of Mormon volunteers. The army was under orders to take possession of New Mexico and move on to California.

In anticipation to his defense of New Mexico, Governor Armijo requested regular troops from Mexico. He received a promise that they would be sent but they never arrived. Meanwhile, he prepared. Standing alone, his militia would be severely outnumbered and underequipped. Many of his men did not have firearms. Instead they had spears, bows, and arrows. And most of the firearms they had were outmoded. They did have the advantage of defending home terrain. The governor formed his defense at Apache Canyon, today's Cañoncito, where the Santa Fe Trail passed through a narrow crevice.

Then two important events took place. The Americans captured one of Armijo's spies. Instead of punishing him, Kearny had him escorted to see the whole army so that he could accurately, and in awe, describe to the governor what he was facing. Next, Kearny sent James Magoffin, an experienced trader in Mexico, along with Captain Philip St. George Cooke and twelve dragoons to meet with the governor. They arrived in Santa Fe on the 12th of August under a flag of truce. Manuel Alvarez arranged the meeting with the governor and his officials. Apparently already aware of the size and equipment of the invading army, Alvarez later wrote that all the governmental officials except the governor were convinced to avoid the disastrous defeat that would follow if they attempted a futile defense.

Governor Armijo did not change his mind until he realized that the promised reinforcements would not arrive in time and after he heard from his commanders in a meeting out on the field. Everyone involved understood that their position at Apache Canyon would only delay the inevitable. Governor Armijo issued the orders to his militia to disband and return to their homes. The governor immediately fled into Mexico, where he had a hand in saving Magoffin's life. Magoffin had been captured and condemned to death in Chihuahua but Armijo successfully interceded on the old merchant's behalf.

Eventually, Armijo returned to the land of his birth to live out the rest of his life in the Rio Abajo. Unfortunately, his life's history has been vilified over the years, culminating in the 1960s, over a century after his last official act, in an interpretation of his actions as those of a dishonest coward who betrayed his people. This apocryphal history portrayed him as a man who abandoned the defense of New Mexico against the Americans because he accepted a $60,000 bribe from Magoffin. No evidence has ever surfaced to remotely verify such a conclusion. None of the people involved with trying to convince Armijo to surrender mentioned a bribe at all. Quite the opposite, they concluded that Armijo was the only official who would not be convinced.

Kearny's army marched into Las Vegas and then Santa Fe. The general made public speeches in both cities, where he promised the local inhabitants that they would be treated as United States citizens.

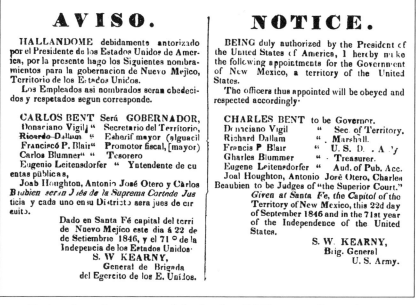

AVISO.

HALLANDOME debidamente antorizado por el Presidente de los Estados Unidos de America, por la presente hago los Siguientes nombramientos para la gobernacion de Nuevo Mejico, Territorio de los Estados Unidos.

Los Empleados asi nombrados seran obedecidos y respetados segun corresponde.

CARLOS BENT Será GOBERNADOR,
Donaciano Vigil " Secretario del Territorio,
Ricardo Dallum " Esherif mayor (alguacil
Francisco P. Blair" Promotor fiscal, [mayor)
Carlos Blumner" " Tesorero
Eugenio Leitensdorfer " Yntendente de cu
entas públicas,
Joab Houghton, Antonio José Otero y Cárlos Brubien seran Jues de la Suprema Cortede Jus ticia y cada uno en su Districto sera jues de cir euito.

Dado en Santa Fé capital del terri de Nuevo Mejico este dia á 22 de de Setiembre 1846, y el 71 ° de la Independia de los Estados Unidos·
S. W KEARNY,
General de Brigada del Egercito de los E. Unidos.

NOTICE.

BEING duly authorized by the President of the United States of America, I hereby make the following appointments for the Government of New Mexico, a territory of the United States.

The officers thus appointed will be obeyed and respected accordingly·

CHARLES BENT to be Governor.
Donaciano Vigil " Sec. of Territory.
Richard Dallam " Marshall.
Francis P Blair " U. S. D . A .y
Charles Blummer " Treasurer.
Eugene Leitensdorfer " Aud. of Pub. Acc.
Joal Houghton, Antonio Jorè Otero, Charles Beaubien to be Judges of "the Superior Court."

Given at Santa Fe, the Capitol of the Territory of New Mexico, this 22d day of September 1846 and in the 71st year of the Independence of the United States.

S. W. KEARNY,
Brig. General
U. S. Army.

Notice of appointments made by Stephen W. Kearny, 22 September 1846. Original in the New Mexico State Records Center and Archives. From Myra Ellen Jenkins and Albert H. Schroeder, A Brief History of New Mexico *(Albuquerque: University of New Mexico Press, 1974).*

They and their customs would be respected. He pointed out that he had Catholics among his own troops. Neither Kearny nor his country could live up to his promise, however, for war continued to rage in Mexico and not every New Mexican was ready to surrender to a foreign occupying force.

Nevertheless, Kearny apparently expressed a personally sincere sentiment. He immediately put people to work to write a code of laws under which everyone could feel comfortable. The *Organic Act*, or, as it came to be called, *The Kearny Code*, was printed and published in English and Spanish. It was a remarkably liberal and humane code for the time and circumstance. Unfortunately, the United States Congress refused to accept the wisdom of Kearny's action and charged him with exceeding his authority. Had they not needed him militarily, for he had embarked for California, the ultimate goal, the president or Congress probably would have reprimanded him.

Kearny left New Mexico under marshal law and took the southern route to California, where he almost lost his life in the Battle of San Pascual, but survived to successfully capture the future west coast state. The Mormon battalion followed, taking supply wagons, thus becoming the first people to take wagons through the southwestern deserts to California.

Meanwhile, resistance broke out in northern New Mexico in Mora, Arroyo Hondo, Embudo, and Taos. On 19 January 1847, Charles Bent, who had been appointed the civil governor under the military, was killed along with some others. The U.S. Army marched north through the snow to put down the rebellion. They fought their way through the pass leading into Embudo, present-day Dixon, and at Taos succeeded in surrounding the Mexican resisters, who were inside the adobe church at Taos Pueblo.

With the help of howitzers fired at very close range, many of the Mexican patriots were killed and a few were captured and tried for treason under circumstances that were less than just. In December and January an estimated 102 Americans and their sympathizers along with 318 Mexican and Indian resisters were killed or wounded.

A teenager from New England arrived in Taos in time to witness the trials. Lewis H. Garrard had traveled west for his health and wrote his impressions of what he saw in Taos.

> When the concluding words *"muerto, muerto, muerto"*—
> dead, dead, dead—were pronounced . . . the painful
> stillness that reigned in the courtroom and the subdued
> grief manifested by a few bystanders were noticed not
> without an inward sympathy. . . . I left the room sick at
> heart. Justice! Out upon the word, when it's distorted
> meaning is the warrant for murdering those who defend
> to the last their country and their homes.

Garrard would take his travel notes and eventually publish them for posterity. In time, even the military questioned itself. Farther Martínez and Manuel Alvarez actually questioned the legality of trying, convicting, and executing men, as indeed some fifteen had been, who defended their homeland against an invading force during a time of war. The inquiry went to Washington, D.C., where neither the president nor his secretary of state had an answer. This was a legal as well as moral question that is still debated.

In fact, this question was raised as a defense in a subsequent trial of seventy-five-year-old Antonio Maria Trujillo. The prosecuting attorney heard the defense's argument and agreed, thus answering the question at the time. The military in New Mexico followed up with a decision that the politicians in Washington refused to touch: resisters could not be charged for treason and all executions would stop.

One of the ironies of the resistance was that the Indians from Taos Pueblo played a major part. This might have happened out of a sense of revenge rather than patriotism for Mexico. Just three years earlier, Taos Pueblo had suffered the brunt of casualties when the Texans ambushed Captain Lobato's contingent. The memory of that loss remained fresh in the minds of the Taos people. It is quite possible that in their minds they associated the Texans with the Americans now occupying the territory. So they took their revenge.

The war did not end until 1848 with the Treaty of Guadalupe Hidalgo. To return to the analogy of the day of a wedding, the war ended the Mexican period with a shot-gun wedding. To be sure, there were some people in all the involved societies—Hispanic, Anglo-American (here is a good place to introduce the Spanish term *estadounidense* (United States citizen), and Native American—who desired this union. After all, interaction and cooperation begun over the Santa Fe Trail had helped prepare people for the moment. Nonetheless, as in any wedding, the real work began after the nuptials.

William S. Messervy, ca. 1849, just off the Santa Fe Trail, from quarter-plate daguerreotype. Photograph courtesy Palace of the Governors (MNM/DCA 88121).

Manifest Destiny and Neo-Aztecism

HORATIO ALGER
MEETS PACO

୭୧

Resistance ended any chance at immediate, stable civil government in New Mexico. Instead, it raised questions about human rights under the United States Constitution and debate about the limits of the military rule that continued after the end of the war. The United States inherited and helped create legal problems and cultural conflicts, and its tenuous military rule appointed an unpopular, subservient civil government that omitted influential leading local personages. Uncertainty reigned and gave rise to political parties or factions. Rivalries, real as well as imagined, created a potential for chaos. As one person put it, "savage Indians, the treacherous Mexicans, and the outlawed Americans" made him feel as though he were sitting on top of a boiling volcano. A recent arrival from the United States noted that the U.S. soldiers had degenerated into a military mob. He charged that the military's appointed officials were corrupt. Probably most everyone at the time could commiserate with the individual who wrote, "Everybody and everything in this . . . country appears at cross purposes."

The political factions generally formed two groups: an antimilitary, pro-statehood faction and a pro-military, territorial faction. The statehood advocates were largely former Mexican citizens along with some Americans who were longtime Santa Fe Trail merchants. The Territorialists represented mostly recently arrived Americans along with a few Mexican merchants. Motives varied, but personal advancement and influence cannot be overlooked. If statehood could be achieved, then all the governmental offices with their subsequent patronage would be filled locally. And the Mexican population outnumbered the newcomers by far, so the implication was that they would get the jobs. If the area became a territory, however, the political leadership positions would be appointed from Washington, D.C., and the newcomers would have the advantage.

Using authority granted under the Kearny Code, a series of New Mexican assemblies were formed to represent New Mexico. A memorial was sent to Congress asking for territorial status with a local legislature and a delegate to Congress, and that slavery be prohibited in New Mexico. The statehood faction passed a memorial in which statehood was requested. They used Missouri's state constitution as a model for New Mexico.

The United States Congress itself became embroiled in the fruits of the recently concluded war, for, along with New Mexico, the politicians had to figure out what to do with California, Arizona, and the Mormons in Utah. Within twelve years of the outbreak of the Civil War, the nation's leaders were grappling with the issue of maintaining, or not, a strong union of states. The heart of that issue was slavery. State's rights advocates maintained that states should determine whether they were free or slave, while unionists claimed that the federal government should make the determination.

New Mexico's status was considered within that national context. Here was a newly annexed region with a population that was neither English-speaking nor Protestant but had a large enough population to qualify for statehood under the United States Constitution. The inhabitants appeared, both to Easterners and to Congress, to be more like Indians than not. Obviously, these "colored" people could not be capable of full state status and the territorial advocates painted that picture to Congress.

Thus, in the Compromise of 1850 brokered by Henry Clay, Daniel Webster, and John C. Calhoun, California and Utah became states while Arizona was added to the Territory of New Mexico. So the honeymoon was over and the marriage would begin.

But there was something deeper at play here. Unknown to all the participants, they were acting out a scenario embedded in the histories of their respective heritages. They lived and acted out of motives born in cultures formed over centuries. Their performances completed an act of history's grand scheme that is our inheritance today.

These motives are best described under the headings of Manifest Destiny, which has been explained above, and Neo-Aztecism, a concept developed in Mexico that paralleled the American concept of the Puritan Ethic, out of which the idea of Manifest Destiny evolved.

If one were to observe a map of North America, including Mexico, and begin to sketch the movements of the British and Spanish societies that settled there, an obvious conclusion would come into focus. New Mexico, at the precise time of the Compromise of 1850, had come to an important historical moment.

British society (and, for argument's sake, let us include the Dutch, French, French Huguenots, Hessians, etc.) settled on the eastern seaboard in North America. From the seeds of a few seventeenth-century colonies in the cold Northeast that they named New England and in the warmer "middle" colonies, such as Virginia and the Carolinas, they expanded west. These religious separatists (although they claimed the opposite) and merchant adventurers began a societal movement that first spread up and down the Atlantic coast and up rivers to the fall lines, that place above which they could not take seafaring ships. Then, some people, who at the time were deemed adventurous if not insane, moved above the fall line, then through the mountains and eventually into the Ohio and Mississippi river valleys. There the people settled but still looked west. Eventually they expanded to, roughly, the 98th degree longitude, where trees quit growing and the plains began. They called the great expanse of treeless land the Great American Desert, for it posed a challenge to the descendants of northern Europe. The people had never experienced life without trees or access to great rivers upon which they could travel to a nearby ocean. At that time they did not have the technology to live on the plains, so, still drawn west, they skipped across the plains to the more inviting coastal environments of California and Oregon. Eventually, when technology allowed it, they bounced back to the plains in the last quarter of the nineteenth century.

The culmination of the Mexican War and the subsequent Compromise of 1850 seemed to fulfill America's destiny. God, many would claim, had rewarded American ingenuity, grit, persistence, and work ethic. The United States had become a transcontinental nation. Within a century it would become a transcontinental world power.

The drive to this destiny was encapsulated in the Puritan Ethic begun by those who first settled in the Northeast. They consciously attempted to set an example for the rest of mankind. Their "beacon on the hill" would show the way to an elevated, God-respecting society and set an example for a decadent Europe. In the process, they created a national mindset. As late as the twentieth century schoolchildren pointedly received this message through the medium of Horatio Alger stories. Alger was a rags-to-riches account of a boy who, through living a Christian life, hard work, and a little good fortune, received God's reward with material success. This message became the openly stated national story as the country expanded east to west and James K. Polk campaigned on the idea of America's Manifest Destiny.

Yet, at the same time and on the same continent, Catholic Europeans from Spain, and others along with them, settled in central Mexico. Over the course of three-plus centuries they too expanded into the continent, but from the south to the north. And they formed a new identity as they expanded and underwent some of the same experiences as their North American counterparts. They also crossed deserts, encountered new peoples, discovered natural wealth, and changed because of their experience. From the beginning of their American experience, many leaders, including Hernán Cortés, the most famous of conquistadores, openly stated that they wanted to create a new and improved society over that left behind in Europe. The philosophy of the very first missionaries, starting with the Franciscans and intellectualized by the Jesuits, saw God's approval imprinted upon this new society with the imprimatur of Neo-Aztecism in the eighteenth century. In books like Francisco Clavijero's *La Historia Antigua de Mexico*, they simply stated that in America they could take the best of European society and the best of the inherited Native American societies to weld a new improved society. Their view was less individualistic and more inclusive. They did not measure morality with material rewards or even anything tangible. Rather, they stressed an eternal reward through good works.

Neo-Aztecism expanded with society from the south to the north, where it came into contact and conflict with the east-to-west movement of the Puritan Ethic. Quite literally, Horatio Alger met Paco, and the focal point of that meeting was in New Mexico, where the farthest northern expansion existed and where, almost as if fate willed it, the Santa Fe Trail connected to the Chihuahua Trail.

This meeting had its irony, for these two movements had their impetus in England and Spain far back in the sixteenth century with the birth of the Reformation. The two "mother countries" had become rivals in Europe as lead countries on opposite sides of the Reformation, one of the great upheavals of western history.

England led the Reformation, especially under Queen Elizabeth I, and Spain under Carlos I (also known as Carlos V, the Holy Roman Emperor) and his son Felipe II led the Counter-Reformation. This rivalry lasted centuries, and its bitterness remained evident in the rivals' American descendants centuries later. Some would argue that the cultural baggage from the sixteenth century still exists today. Certainly, unbeknown to the people then, these prejudices existed in the middle of the nineteenth century. And New Mexico, as the hub of this re-encounter, became an important point of interest from which lessons can be learned for the benefit of everyone.

The Elsberg & Amberg Wagon Train in Santa Fe's plaza, October 1861.
Photograph courtesy Palace of the Governors (MNM/DCA 11254).

CHAPTER SEVEN

A New Age

TERRITORIAL
NEW MEXICO

☙❧

The territorial period of New Mexico's history lasted 62 years, from 1850 until 1912, when New Mexico became a state. After over 250 years of living under Spanish and then Mexican rule, New Mexicans now lived under an English-speaking government housed in Washington, D.C. So a primarily Spanish-speaking populace would need to adapt to different attitudes, laws, and customs. The territorial years represent a period of New Mexico's history in which varied peoples of New Mexico, now united, would learn to live together and, like in any nuptial, the parties did not always agree.

This societal accommodation can be seen in the change of legal systems, religion, and Indian policy. The change in legal systems is especially evident in the area of landownership and water rights, still being litigated today. The new American Catholic Church superimposed itself on the

Mexican church and the penitent brotherhoods went secretive. Indian policies, along with military strength, ended raiding and confined tribes to reservations, which were a new innovation and, in New Mexico, were mostly on traditional lands. The constant struggle for statehood reflected the struggle of the new society that evolved.

One underlining trend, begun in earlier periods, and a problem still unresolved in the minds of many, gained notoriety during the territorial years. The legal issue of landownership as it was transferred from the Spanish/Mexican system to being recognized under the United States' legal system became a subject of controversy. Article X of the Treaty of Guadalupe Hidalgo specifically protected landownership for former Mexican citizens who resided in the territories that had become United States possessions as a result of the Mexican War. While the United States Senate eliminated Article X from the treaty, the Mexican government secured an agreement to include a supplemental document known as a "protocol" that allowed recipients of land grants to bring their cases before American tribunals for ratification. The final Treaty of Guadalupe Hidalgo, with its protocol, acknowledged that the property of Mexicans had to be respected.

Property rights became a little less clear when the southern limits of the United States' territory came under debate. Negotiations resulted in the ratification of the Gadsden Purchase in December of 1853. This treaty defined a new southern border, which has lasted until the present. Still, the new border was not without problems. This border extended west to the Colorado River, just above its mouth. This meant that the Colorado River would empty in Mexican territory and lead to subsequent international disagreements. A second curious problem with the Gadsden Purchase had to do with a small number of Mexican citizens who chose to leave New Mexico after the Mexican War. These people moved to what they considered Mexican territory in the Mesilla Valley around present-day Las Cruces. However, the 1853 action placed them again in the United States. The story of these people and what became of them has yet to be told.

Within a year of the Gadsden Purchase, the U.S. Congress created the Office of Surveyor General of New Mexico to determine all claims of land under the "laws, usages, and customs of Spain and Mexico." The surveyor general would submit his findings to the secretary of interior, who, upon review, submitted them to Congress for final action.

Unfortunately, the system did not work. The surveyor general quickly learned that the locals could not afford to file as well as pay for the procedure. In addition, a great many people had no confidence that they would get a fair hearing, even to the point that they feared losing original documents to the American officials and thus losing any chance of keeping their land. Then, as the first surveyor general put it, lawyers, "designing individuals," who had political connections completely corrupted the system. "Adventurers of every description," mostly lawyers and politicians, descended on the territory seeking land. The Office of Surveyor General aligned with the lawyers for mutual gain, the result of which was many fraudulent claims, misrepresentation, and the disenfranchisement of landownership from Mexican landowners. A little more than 25 percent of the non-Indian claims for land were confirmed by 1879, and none after that.

The Civil War came to New Mexico in 1861–62. The Confederacy needed to defeat Union resistance in New Mexico to get to the recently discovered silver of Colorado. The seaports of California also beckoned and New Mexico stood between the Confederacy and California.

Southern New Mexico sided with the Confederacy, while northern New Mexico remained loyal to the Union. The invading Confederate army marched out of Texas through El Paso and north into New Mexico, where it defeated its first resistance at Fort Craig south of Socorro. The "Texans," as they were called in New Mexico, then occupied Albuquerque and Santa Fe. The big test came when they met troops primarily from Fort Union, but also including New Mexico volunteers and a newly arrived contingent from Colorado. The culminating battle took place on the Santa Fe Trail at Glorieta Canyon. The Confederates could not breach the Union defenses and when their supply train was ambushed and sacked they had no choice but to retreat south.

The Civil War even disrupted the land shenanigans, but after the war they continued anew. From 1869 to 1884 an estimated 67 percent of the five-year homesteads granted in New Mexico were fraudulent. Once the claims passed from Hispanic ownership the system was used to increase the size and value of the land. Such exaggerated land grant claims also confused the issue.

Grant claims grew to as large as 2 million acres for an individual grant, even though the secretary of interior limited the claims to a maximum of 97,000 acres, which was the maximum under Mexican law. George Julian, probably the only honest surveyor general, blamed the problem on land speculators who "hovered over the territory like a pestilence" and "subordinated everything to greed for land." No wonder the locals had no confidence in the system.

Eventually, even the politicians in Washington, D.C. heard enough complaints coming out of New Mexico. In May 1891 Congress took action and, at once, closed the Office of Surveyor General and created the Court of Private Land Claims. The court organized in Denver of that same year and completed its work in June 1904, a little over thirteen years later.

The new legislation moved the land question from the political realm to the courtroom. Congress hoped to solve a problem that previous legislation had failed to settle. Part of the act even stated that Congress had ruled on questions about which it knew nothing. So the new system called before it all unresolved claims as well as what were described as legitimate claims under Spanish and Mexican law. Once again, though, defining "legitimate" and then proving the fact in the American legal system proved illusive to many Hispanic landowners. Although the blatant illegal activities of earlier were abated, the question of landownership still could not be resolved—and the problem exists today.

∞

The people who dominated the land question became known as the Santa Fe Ring. They were a loosely connected group of men, most of whom moved into the area after the change of administrations. They came together over mutual interests, were not formerly organized, and used the confused legal status of land and other matters in New Mexico to their advantage. They garnered wealth as well as influence and used the time and place as an opportunity to advance themselves. They became associated with the railroads, mining, government contracts, and cattle companies, as well as land speculation.

The names most associated with the Santa Fe Ring were congressional delegates and lawyers such as Stephen B. "Smooth Steve" Elkins, who was from Virginia originally; Antonio Joseph; and Thomas B. Catron, who came to New Mexico at the insistence of his Missouri law school classmate, Elkins. Governor Samuel B. Axtell is especially noted for his lack of scruples and for his total ignorance of and appreciation for history. He was the governor who used centuries-old Spanish documents for kindling in the Palace of the Governors. At one time he even tossed a bunch of documents out onto the street in front of the palace. A casual passerby found them scattered about and had sense enough to collect them. Those saved documents form the core of the Spanish Archives in New Mexico's State Records Center and Archives today. One wonders if Governor Axtell's disdain for the archives had to do with the matter of encountering definitive proof of land ownership that ran contrary to the Ring's interests.

L. Bradford Prince, also a territorial governor, did not share Axtell's disregard for New Mexico's history, for he helped reform the Historical Society of New Mexico and wrote some history books about New Mexico. Yet, his appetite for land speculations and accumulated wealth allied him with the Ring. Both Axtell and Prince began their support for the Ring as federal judges, which hints at the close ties between the Ring and the Republican Party through federal patronage.

The Ring's activities resulted in protest and opposition. The Gorras Blancas, hooded nightriders who cut fences and burned barns, are a prime example. Their activities grew out of a rural Hispanic New Mexican sense of helplessness at the loss of their lands. The gunfighter Clay Allison, in Cimarron, also rode in opposition to the Ring, whose henchmen had terrified and then burned down the town's opposition newspaper. The periodical's printing press was tossed into the Cimarron River, never to be found again.

Even New Mexico's most famous desperado, Billy the Kid, achieved his notoriety mostly fighting against the Ring's interests after his unarmed boss was ambushed and gunned down. The real issue was not who killed whom, for the cowboys-turned-gunmen were all pawns in a larger commercial struggle. The Lincoln County War, in which Billy the Kid, John Henry Tunstall, and John Chisum participated, was over who would control government contracts to feed the Mescalero Apaches on their nearby reservation. The contracts were lucrative and the Indians easy to cheat—the Mescaleros rarely received the food due to them.

Lew Wallace, governor of New Mexico and author. From Ralph Emerson Twitchell, Old Santa Fe: The Story of New Mexico's Ancient Capital *(Santa Fe: The Santa Fe New Mexico Publishing Corporation, 1925).*

So the Santa Fe Ring and those connected to them used whatever means available, including murder, to achieve their ends. Naturally, people fought back, and the whole image of a corrupt and violent land did much to forestall statehood.

Two governors stand out during this period. Lew Wallace was a lawyer from Indiana who became a Union general during the Civil War. He was appointed territorial governor, presumably as a reward for his military service, although it was mediocre at best. He would go on to be a United States ambassador to the Middle East, but what he is most noted for is that he wrote *Ben Hur*, the first biblical novel in United States literary history. He finished the book while resident in Santa Fe's Palace of the Governors.

Wallace had traveled to New Mexico with instructions to stop the lawlessness in the territory. He replaced Governor Axtell and in fact was there partly because of his predecessor's poor performance. He arrived at a time when the Lincoln County War was at its worst, and his most noteworthy act was his offer of general amnesty to all of the war's participants, including Billy the Kid, if they stopped fighting. Everyone accepted the offer, but old habits and hatreds are hard to change. The fighting and killing began anew.

Pat Garrett eventually hunted down and killed the Kid after the latter had escaped from jail, killing two lawmen in the process. Garrett, one of the West's honest lawmen, was killed while bringing in a Santa Fe Ring gunman who had been charged for murder. So, Governor Wallace, whose dislike for New Mexico was surpassed only by his wife's, left New Mexico without any significant political accomplishment.

Edmund Ross, the first governor appointed by a Democrat president, was a different story. His fame came when he, as a U.S. Senator, cast the deciding vote against the impeachment of President Andrew Johnson. That decision cost him his political career, so he moved to Albuquerque, New Mexico, to open a store. But President Grover Cleveland, the only Democrat elected between the Civil War and the end of the century, appointed the ex-senator to be governor of New Mexico.

Ross had nothing good to say about the Santa Fe Ring. He understood the power of these ambitious and corrupt men. Ross agreed with John Henry Tunstall, who wrote, "everything in New Mexico that pays at all is worked by a 'ring.'" With more experience, Ross was able to describe the situation more succinctly:

> Many years ago a few sharp shrewd Americans came
> here—discovered a number of small Mexican and
> Spanish Grants—purchased them at nominal prices—
> learned the Spanish language—ingratiated themselves
> into favor with the Mexican people, and proceeded
> to enlarge the Grants they had purchased, and
> to manufacture at will, titles to still others, and to
> secure therefore Congressional recognition.

Yet he determined to reform the territorial system, thus maintaining the "profile in courage" bestowed upon him years later by John F. Kennedy in his Pulitzer Prize–winning book. Ross did succeed in slowing the corruption. After his death, he was buried in Albuquerque's Fairview Cemetery, where he remains today virtually unknown.

∞

Hoping to solidify their landholdings and political stature, the members of the Santa Fe Ring worked for statehood. New Mexico had lost its initial attempt at statehood as its request became entangled in the slavery issue. Then the Civil War broke out, after which reconstruction had stymied any attempts at statehood. The Santa Fe Ring really exerted its influence in the 1870s and 1880s, after the Civil War. Ironically, their own activities in New Mexico—involvement in corruption, lawlessness, disenfranchisement, and violence—created an image that hindered the movement for statehood. In many ways the individuals of the Ring were doing in New Mexico what many reconstructionists were doing in the South. Well-connected men from elsewhere moved into the territory in order to use their influence in Washington to take advantage of locals and garner power and wealth. Stephen B. Elkins was elected to Congress and in 1876 personally lost an opportunity to achieve statehood for New Mexico when he alienated the Southern vote by rushing to shake hands with a representative who had just delivered a tirade in Congress against the South.

Internal indifference also delayed the process. In 1866 a statehood convention dissolved without reaching a quorum. In 1872, the territory failed to approve a proposed progressive state constitution, and in 1889 another proposed constitution lost approval at the polls.

The reasons for the 1889 defeat are illustrative of New Mexico's local problems. The church actively opposed the constitution on the basis of its opposition to public and secular schools. Others joined forces to prevent "land grabbers" from solidifying their power, while others feared increased taxation. Hispanos generally believed that statehood would result in the domination of one group over another and this, too, further complicated the issue of church-state relations.

New Mexico always seemed to be slightly out of step with the national mood. Some powerful senators, especially Indiana's Albert

Santa Fe, New Mexico, looking west, April 1880.
Photograph by Ben Wittick. Courtesy
Palace of the Governors (MNM/DCA 15843).

Beveridge, who chaired the Committee of Territories in the 1890s, opposed the influence of big businesses and foreign investors and landowners in the territory. This, of course, was a criticism of the Santa Fe Ring. Other opposition to New Mexico's petition for statehood ran the gamut from claims that it had too sparse a population, or too arid a climate, to the argument that another western state that would tip one party or another's balance, and so on. And New Mexico's conservatism did not help. Yet other western states such as Colorado, Washington, the Dakotas, and Wyoming, all less populated and some as arid and conservative, achieved statehood.

The real underlying difference between New Mexico and the rest of the western territories was the makeup of its population. Beveridge himself expressed this national and eastern bias on many occasions. Another Congressman shared Beveridge's and the country's prejudices toward Hispanos when he noted that New Mexico's inhabitants were "a race speaking an alien language" who did not represent "the best blood on the American continent." Where Native Americans figured on this scale of Anglo-American superiority is hinted at in the 1853 election of José Manuel Gallegos. Gallegos was an ex-priest from Albuquerque who had run afoul of Lamy and who did not speak English. He successfully defeated the "American" candidate, so his opponents challenged the election in Congress. While not overturning the election, Congress did disallow the Indian vote. A concerted campaign, including some local opposition, the Catholic Church under Archbishop Lamy, and an already hostile Congress eventually removed him from his congressional seat. Congress could not accept either Gallegos or the Indian vote.

∞

From the inception of the territorial years, the Catholic Church had been a source of controversy. Even to this day historians debate the foibles of Archbishop Jean B. Lamy. Within two years of the territory's creation the church followed suit and formed the new Archdiocese of Santa Fe, which included all of New Mexico. The move would assure that the Catholic inhabitants of New Mexico would not have divided loyalties between Mexico and the United States by remaining a part of the Durango diocese.

Then the United States leaders of the Catholic Church appointed Lamy, a Frenchman then working in Ohio, to be the first bishop of the new archdiocese. The reasoning, it seems, was twofold. Reflecting eastern attitudes, the church fathers never considered appointing one of New Mexico's own to the position. Rather, they came up with a compromise in a Frenchman who, they thought, would surely get along with the Mexicans who were Latins like him. They were wrong.

Lamy brought to New Mexico a biased attitude born of his religious and conservative French upbringing. Despite his gracious welcome by the local Mexican priests, led by Vicar Ortiz, his demeanor and actions, as well as those of his assistant and lifelong friend, Jean B. Machebeuf (his surname translates to "beef chewer") alienated the local priests and the Hispanic population. Eventually even the territorial legislature petitioned Rome over the perceived abuses. Machebeuf successfully defended himself in Rome but not without Lamy and him compromising themselves and the truth in his defense.

Lamy became the darling of the Americans, however, even the Protestants, whose missionaries spread out among the Hispanic and Pueblo villages to convert and help "Americanize" them. Subsequent English-speaking authors penned novels and histories extolling the virtues of the good archbishop while denigrating the Mexican clergy who opposed him. Only recently have historians delved into the archives of documents and letters written in Spanish, to reveal the other side of the story.

Those priests who most actively complained and resisted the Lamy administration's anti-Mexican activities and violations of church law received the brunt of the criticism. One was José Manuel Gallegos, who left the church to successfully run for Congress, serve in the territorial legislature, and become an Episcopalian priest. Padre Antonio Martínez of Taos was the most obvious and vociferous opponent of Lamy. While the record shows that Martínez tried to cooperate with Lamy, in the end he and the bishop could not get along. Lamy's boosters used Martínez as Lamy's foil, overlooking his long career in education, training priests, printing New Mexico's first books, and advocating for his community.

Those early church activities illustrate that even at the crux of New Mexico's change from Hispanic Mexican to United States administration, religion played a significant role. The prejudices of the new nation were painfully evident even in its dealings with a specific sect, let alone in its attempts to convert to more nationally accepted sects. The Penitentes' movement to secrecy and their eventual separation from the church is an obvious reaction to this environment. Despite the invitations of current archbishops who are willing to accept the brotherhoods back into the church's fold, some still remain suspicious. And, within New Mexico today, Padre Martínez and Archbishop Lamy remain enigmas. They are both respected and not respected within the respective Hispanic and non-Hispanic communities.

Like Martínez, however, Lamy stressed education. With greater resources than his predecessors, Lamy built schools and personally recruited the Sisters of Loretto to teach at girls' boarding schools first in Santa Fe and, eventually, Mora and Socorro. The issue of education eventually allied the Hispanic community with the church in their opposition to statehood. They both opposed public, secular education, which statehood would establish. Because of the church's opposition and the Hispanic community's suspicion, public education was not established in New Mexico until 1891.

∞

Judaism came to New Mexico with the arrival of a few Ashkenazi Jews. We now know that some of these people were involved with the Santa Fe Trail, but the first openly Jewish people to settle permanently came during and after the Mexican War. Most originated in Eastern Europe, especially the German states, where they left for various political as well as economic reasons. They were part of a larger European migration during the period. Most crossed the Atlantic and settled on the East Coast, but a few, like many other people, saw their opportunity out west.

From the seeds of these few men, not more than twenty initially, these first people who openly acknowledged themselves as Jews gained influence beyond their numbers to become an integral part of the fabric of New Mexican society. They partnered with locals, founded communities, helped establish civic organizations, fought in the Indian and Civil wars, and became community as well as political leaders. This unheralded segment of New Mexico's heritage is only now receiving proper credit.

Yetta Kohn

Yetta Kohn personified New Mexico during the last quarter of the nineteenth century. She was an immigrant, born in Bavaria in 1843 and one of New Mexico's pioneer Jews. Her success illustrates the kind of opportunity the West had for women.

She immigrated to the United States with her family at an early age, under the name Yetta Goldsmith. By 1857, when she was fourteen years old, she was living in Fort Leavenworth, Kansas, where she married Samuel Kohn, also an immigrant German-Jew, from Pilson.

After moving around between Colorado and Kansas, Yetta and Samuel traveled down the Santa Fe Trail to Las Vegas, New Mexico. They arrived in that rough town in the middle of the 1860s and were greeted by the not-so-pleasant sight of some men hanging from the windmill tower in the town's plaza. Las Vegas is said to have hanged more men than any other western town.

Undeterred by this gruesome first impression, the Kohns decided to open a store, in which they sold wood, hides, flour, and grain. By all accounts they prospered, but unfortunately, Samuel died in 1878. He left Yetta with four children and the store.

With true grit, Yetta continued to run the business, but after four years she sold out and moved her family to the village of La Cinta, near the present-day site of Conchas Dam in eastern New Mexico. There she opened another store and expanded her vocations.

She became the village postmistress while running a ferry across the Canadian River. She also saved enough money to begin purchasing small parcels of land. Eventually she and some partners, including her son Howard, daughter Belle, and friends Louis Sulzbacher and Henry Waldo, owned 3,858 head of cattle, which they ran on Yetta's 4V Ranch.

Apparently, enthralled with the idea of moving on to more opportunities, Yetta moved her family to the new town of Montoya, where they purchased a store, opened a bank, and acquired more land. This time they acquired the land through the federal government's Homestead Act.

Yetta Kohn's gumption and hard work helped her to survive. Her life is a part of New Mexico's legacy. Her son Charles participated in New Mexico's Constitutional Convention and her 4V Ranch became the basis of the T-4 Cattle Company, which remains in the family to this day.

Interestingly enough, these Jewish pioneers made no mention of secret Sephardic Jews, who recent historians claim have existed within New Mexico's Hispanic Catholic population. This lack of mention is a question that requires further research. The hidden Jews are alleged to have come to New Mexico with the first Spanish colonists. They were forced to convert to Catholicism or leave their native Spain beginning in the late sixteenth century. Many Jews left Spain rather than convert. Others converted to remain, and still others outwardly converted but secretly maintained and practiced their religion. It is safe to say that many of those who converted, both in sincerity and not, traveled and settled throughout the Spanish empire, where, over the centuries, they mixed with their respective local societies. Today, centuries later, many theories have surfaced in attempts to identify who are the descendents of the converts, or *conversos*, and then to establish who really converted and who did not. That the Spanish Inquisition's most vicious and dogmatic inquisitor general, Tomás de Torquemada, was a descendant of converts would indicate, at minimum, that some of the converted were serious about their conversion. To assume that all conversos secretly remained Jews is as wrong as to assume the opposite.

The fact that nineteenth-century Jews in New Mexico left no indication of encountering secrete brethren, in a day when Jews who openly acknowledged their religion were, by all appearances, accepted into society, raises a historical question that may never be answered. Actually and accurately identifying who, if anyone, in New Mexico was a converso or a descendant of a converso who secretly practiced Judaism is a tall order.

∽

On 19 February 1881 the Atchison, Topeka and Santa Fe Railroad arrived in Santa Fe. The AT&SF traversed northern New Mexico, connecting Chicago to Los Angeles. The Southern Pacific Railroad, traveling across southern New Mexico, connected New Orleans to the Pacific coast. The two rail lines represented two of three transcontinental railroads. Reflecting the area's key geographical position in the national effort to connect with the west coast, both crossed New Mexico between 1879 and

Socorro Courthouse. Painting by Leon Trousset, 1885. Oil on canvas.
Original in the collection of the Museum of Fine Art, Santa Fe, N.Mex.
Gift of John Gaw Meem, 1975.

1881. Railroads signaled a change to the area even more profound than the coming together of New Mexico's varied cultures and societies. Technology cut through all cultures and all lifestyles in the last half of the century.

The innovation of refrigeration gave rise to one of New Mexico's major businesses as well as a romantic lore of the West—the cattle industry and cowboys. Although the Spanish introduced cattle to America and almost every cowboy term (including "buckaroo," an English-speaking simplification of the Spanish *vaquero*, which comes from vaca, "cow," and literally translates as "cowboy"), the combination of refrigeration and the railroad changed the eating habits of the United States from poultry to beef. The now famous cattle drives moved "beef on the hoof" to railheads, where trains transported them to the slaughterhouses in Chicago. From there the butchered product was packed into refrigerated cars to be distributed throughout North America.

Sadie Orchard

Sadie Orchard was born Sadie Jane Creech, probably in Iowa around 1860. She grew up in a large family in Kansas, where she learned all about horses. In her mid-twenties she moved to Kingston, New Mexico. Kingston was established as a wild mining tent city in 1882. By then the town boasted a main street, a few permanent buildings, and seven thousand inhabitants. Desperados, Indian raids, fires, floods, and flu epidemics had become a part of life in the young town.

Within a year Sadie moved to Hillsboro, just eight miles away, which was an older and more established community. The town was a little less dangerous and offered more opportunities. The facts of Sadie's life demonstrate that she had some education, refinement, and a lot of ambition. She also was a compassionate woman who had a temper.

Why she chose prostitution as a vocation is as unknown as why she apparently claimed to be from England and even spoke with an accent. She became successful over the next ten years in her common as well as dangerous vocation. Unlike many women in her profession, she never appeared to be in trouble with the law.

She was not especially good looking and was described as a "fair but frail" woman who stood about five feet tall and did not weigh more than a hundred pounds. She dressed as a Victorian lady with her brunet hair worn up, and every photograph of her mounted on a horse shows her seated sidesaddle. She had an attractive personality that won her friends and influence.

She married James W. Orchard in 1895. James owned and operated the Lake Valley to Kingston Stagecoach Line. Sadie used her familiarity with horses to her advantage with her husband's business. She reputedly helped to break broncos and, on occasion, drove the stagecoaches. The "Mountain Pride" stagecoach, replete with portraits of the Apache leader Victorio on its doors, was the company's pride. At her height, she would have had to stand upright while holding the reins to work the foot-operated brake. The image of her in the "boot," negotiating four to six horses on the many grades and curves of her husband's company route, is the basis for legend. *The Santa Fe New Mexican* newspaper noted that the Orchard stage line had "the best vehicles, best horses and the best looking driver in the Southwest."

Within the next decade she not only helped her husband but she also opened and ran two hotels, at least one of which doubled as a brothel. She built and opened the Ocean Grove Hotel in 1896 and hired

*The "Mountain Pride," Sadie Orchard's stagecoach, at the G. T. Miller
drugstore in Hillsboro, New Mexico, 1905–1908. Photograph by
George T. Miller. Courtesy Palace of the Governors (MNM/DCA 76907).*

Chinese immigrant Tom Ying to be her cook. He became her trusted
business partner and stayed with her for many years. She also opened
the Orchard Hotel shortly thereafter, and was listed as the
"Proprietress" of the Hillsboro Hotel. By 1900, the Orchard Hotel had
become a brothel.

Eventually she and her husband had some problems that resulted
in a messy divorce. For the only time in her life she encountered problems with law enforcement. She was charged and fined for taking a pot-
shot at her husband. Then she was accused of stealing his buggy and of
shooting a deadly weapon. For the rest of her life she kept the Orchard
name and referred to herself as a widow.

Sadie Orchard spent the rest of her life in Hillsboro. In later life,
she is remembered as a pleasant lady who children loved. She may have
adopted a child. She was an individual who cared for the sick and even
helped bury those who died during the flu epidemics that hit the area
in the early part of the twentieth century.

She died in April 1943. A sister and brother attended her funeral in
Hot Springs, now Truth or Consequences. She was not forgotten, for
someone keeps placing flowers on her grave. Perhaps reflecting the
paradoxes of her life, the flowers are taken from other graves in the
cemetery. As historian Erna Fergusson wrote, "For a bad woman, Sadie
was one of the best." And the "Mountain Pride" stagecoach, as well as
her Ocean Grove Hotel, still exist as memorials to her.

The Old Albuquerque Plaza. Painting by Leon Trousset, 1885.
Oil on canvas. Original in the collections of the Albuquerque Museum.
Photograph courtesy the Albuquerque Museum (PC 1976.115.1).

A branch of the Chisum Trail, a cattle-drive route from west Texas, north, cut through eastern New Mexico, eventually to Las Vegas. That town became the largest city in New Mexico, surpassing both Santa Fe and the newly burgeoning Albuquerque as the commercial center for the territory.

Weaponry progressed from single-shot percussion firearms to multi-fire six-shooters and Winchester rifles. The telegraph, electricity, the telephone, and even recording devices came to New Mexico before the end of the century. Technology provided the means for a mining boom that extracted all kinds of minerals. And most of the mines needed trains to transport their product to market. As a result, over 80 percent of all railroad tracks were laid in New Mexico between 1880 and 1900.

Even seemingly ordinary innovations like the introduction of tin would change New Mexico's architecture and art. Finally, the easy transport of glass for windows, replacing the age-old use of mica, wood shutters, or leather hangings, had a profound impact in New Mexico.

∞

As far back as the Mexican period, people traveled west for their health. Richard Henry Dana boarded a "Yankee Clipper," sailed to San Francisco, and published his account in *Two Years Before the Mast.* A year earlier, in 1846, Hector Lewis Garrard (alias Lewis H. Garrard), just seventeen years old, left his native Cincinnati, Ohio, to travel down the Santa Fe Trail to Taos and Santa Fe. As one historian said, his "lack of a stout constitution" was one reason for his trip. He published his account, *Wah-to-Yah and the Taos Trail, etc.,* in 1850.

With a national outbreak of tuberculosis (TB) and no real cures developed, a belief, begun in Germany, in "climate therapy" encouraged "lungers," as they were called, to seek climates that offered combinations of pure air, high altitudes for lower air pressure, plenty of sun, and dryness. An article in an 1898 publication of *The Journal of the American Medical Association* stated that "there does not exist a better or more ideal climate for the elimination of disease and the restoration of health" than New Mexico. That article repeated what many people, including doctors, already surmised, for by the end of the nineteenth century lungers and their relatives had become a significant portion of the territory's population.

New Mexico's health industry grew to proportions beyond most other states. The afflicted and their relatives who had moved to New Mexico had a major impact on society. For example, a young Dr. William Randolph Lovelace moved to New Mexico, became cured, and eventually founded what became the Lovelace Medical Center. U.S. Senators Bronson Cutting and Clinton P. Anderson, along with Albuquerque City Manager and New Mexico Governor Clyde Tingley, among many other political leaders, came to New Mexico because of TB. Others, like Dr. France Scholes, one of New Mexico's greatest historians and dean of the University of New Mexico's graduate school, and John Gaw Meem, a famous southwestern architect, also moved to the area for health reasons. U.S. Representative Albert G. Simms not only served the state politically but also fathered a family still making a huge impact on the state. The impact of these turn-of-the-century health seekers cannot be overlooked.

∞

In most respects Native Americans, New Mexico's original peoples, faired the worst of all. As mentioned, they lost the right to vote almost immediately at the beginning of the territorial period. On the other hand, among the Native American groups the Pueblo Indians had the least trouble keeping the basis of their land. Spanish and then Mexican policy determined that each of the pueblos had specified land grants plus pasturage. The king of Spain, through his New Mexican governors, actually acknowledged the Pueblos as subjects of the Crown who were entitled to govern themselves. As a symbol of this special acknowledgment he gave the governors of each pueblo a cane of office. President Abraham Lincoln followed this practice by also giving each governor a new cane of office. The Pueblos kept their Spanish grants, though extended lands for pasturage or religious purposes as well as water rights came under question.

The non-Pueblo Indians, who continued raiding into the territorial years, did not fair as well. In the south, Mescalero, San Marcos, and Chiricahua Apaches continued raiding, while to the west and north the Navajos and Utes did the same. The United States Army, now at strength because of the Civil War, and with a recent influx of black companies (the buffalo soldiers), turned its attention on the raiders, who refused to adapt to the foreign lifestyle on reservations. The Jicarilla Apaches in north-central New Mexico are an exception. As longtime allies with the Spanish and Mexican administrations who had moved off the plains to begin farming in the early eighteenth century, they were prepared to accept their land in the mountains of northern New Mexico.

The United States government experiment at Fort Sumner, where Mescalero and Navajo Indians were forced to live and farm, was a dismal failure that made the reservation system look good in comparison. Neither tribe was prepared for the shock of such a change. Resistance by the Apaches did not end until the 1880s, when Native leaders like Geronimo, Victorio, Mangas Colorado, and Cochise either were subdued or agreed to peace. Technology and numbers of replaceable

"Old Loco—One Eye Lost," chief of the Warm Springs Apache.
Photograph by Ben Wittick. Courtesy Palace of the
Governors (MNM/DCA 76905).

soldiers as well as the influence of new people moving into the area, it is clear, defeated the last of the militant resistance. But Native resistance or, more aptly stated, the pursuit of Native rights and cultural preservation, continues today.

American Indian culture has become a major, if not obvious, part of the United States' western folklore and romanticism. This began in the last half of the nineteenth century and the railroads were the catalyst. Easy and quick transportation gave rise to the Wild West shows, took Indian delegations to the East, and transported people to the

Adolph Bandelier, archaeologist and historian, ca. 1885.
Photograph courtesy Palace of the Governors (MNM/DCA 9144).

West who were eager to learn about, as well as buy up, Native American culture, arts, and crafts.

The academic community took an intellectual interest in these "ancient people." In 1893 the Frederick E. Hyde Foundation in New York City sent anthropologists and archaeologists to New Mexico to study and collect from various tribes. All the collections, notes, and records went to the American Museum of Natural History in New York. The Hyde Expedition was one of many such "studies" that extracted artifacts and information and deposited it out of the state.

The father of southwestern archaeology, the Swiss-born Adolph Bandelier (after whom a national monument is named on the Pajarito Plateau near Los Alamos) initiated the study of Native Americans, which is still a prominent field in academia. Another archaeologist, Edgar Lee Hewitt, founded the School of American Research in 1909, which, in turn, gave birth to the Museum of New Mexico in the same year. Hewitt went on to become the president of the recently established New Mexico Normal School, now New Mexico Highlands University in Las Vegas. He also oversaw the construction and installation of New Mexico's contribution to the Panama-Pacific International Exposition in San Diego, California. That building became the architectural prototype for the Fine Arts Museum that Hewitt would build in Santa Fe in 1917. Both buildings still exist.

Native Americans became a tourist attraction for the railroad's associated hotels. The Harvey Houses used their specially trained "Harvey Girls" to conduct tours to Indian pueblos and ceremonials. Markets for Indian pottery, weaving, and jewelry, whether traditional or not, developed at each of the train stops. Not surprisingly, entrepreneurs opened curio stores, first in the towns, and then in trading posts out on the reservations. One of the most successful businessmen, Charles Ilfeld, even hired Indians to make Indian jewelry that was not limited to Indian motifs.

Oliver LaFarge won a Pulitzer Prize for his 1929 novel *Laughing Boy*, about pre-contact Indians living on the Pajarito Plateau. Charles Lummis, an easterner who walked across the continent, eventually to settle in Los Angeles and write about his experience, took famous photographs of Adolph Bandelier's excavations as well as of Indian ceremonials. He, like other photographers working in the area, created a

sensation with his images. Imagine, for example, the reaction of an easterner upon seeing an image of Hopi Indian snake dancers. Lummis
became one of the founders of Los Angeles's Southwest Museum.

But tribes have imposed limits on invasions of their privacy. Like
the Penitentes, the tribes began to resent the attention brought to them.
They did not appreciate being mere curiosities. They had their own religions. They had spent centuries adjusting to Hispanic culture and had
achieved a balance. Now a new society had its own ideas and missionaries. Their influence was more pervasive. So, in an attempt to maintain
their cultures, tribes began to withdraw, and to limit what the public
could see and use. Certain rites, activities, and places were sacred, or at
least private. This protectionism came under the rubric of Native
American autonomy. And, again, the struggle over culture continues.

∞

As disarrayed and dangerous as New Mexico appeared, the place was
becoming a destination point. Even New Mexicans, although somewhat
hesitantly on the part of some, began to self-promote. Taking the
lead from Philadelphia's Centennial Celebration in 1876, the territory's
leaders organized a major exposition in Santa Fe in 1883. New Mexico's
exposition celebrated the tertio-millennial anniversary. The tertio-mil-
lennium, or 333rd anniversary, dated back to 1550, a year in which nothing of any known historical importance occurred in New Mexico.
Nevertheless, the name sounded good and was a good excuse to hold a
party. And the idea of an exposition reflected a previously unexpressed
interest in the area's heritage.

The exposition's grounds were developed two blocks north of
the capital's main plaza. A newly graded oval racetrack circled the exhibition halls and the exposition's grounds. Remnants of that track
are still evident in the roads circling today's federal courthouse and
post office building.

Each county presented a display about itself. Parades as well as
special dinners, dances, and concerts were held. The parades functioned
as pageants with themes featuring the Native American, Hispanic, and
Anglo cultures. The different pueblos represented themselves with
dances and music. Men dressed up in historically inaccurate Spanish

*Bridge Street looking east in Las Vegas, New Mexico, ca. 1892.
Photograph courtesy Palace of the Governors (MNM/DCA 14720).*

costumes and armor. A procession of these men, representing Vargas and his historic *entrada*, rode into town from Rosario Chapel, which was Vargas's old campsite of many years ago, to the plaza. Early pioneers from the United States received attention in other processions.

The Tertio-millennial Exposition took the already existing Indian dances and Catholic processions, especially La Conquistadora's annual novena processions, and morphed them into Santa Fe's famous annual fiestas.

∞

This popular interest in history had expressed itself two years earlier, in 1881, with the rebirth of the Historical Society of New Mexico. The HSNM had an earlier start in 1859, only to be overwhelmed by the Civil War. Today, it is the oldest historical society west of the Mississippi River.

Within the next ten years the New Mexico College of Agriculture and Mechanic Arts (1888), the University of New Mexico (1889), and the New Mexico Normal School would be established. New Mexico State University grew out of the first college, and New Mexico Highlands University came from the New Mexico Normal School. Interestingly enough, the roots of the College of Santa Fe, a private Catholic college, predate the area's public institutions as well as the establishment of public education. The College of Santa Fe, then known as St. Michael College, started as a Christian Brothers boarding school for secondary education, in 1874 and became a four-year institution in 1947.

∞

In 1898 the United States went to war with Spain. This was the second war in which New Mexico participated during the territorial period, which, in reality, had begun with a third. The Spanish-American War of 1898 offered another opportunity for New Mexico to demonstrate its loyalty and possibly win support for statehood in Congress. Theodore "Teddy" Roosevelt sent out a call for volunteers throughout the West. He proposed to form a regiment of horsemen, cowboys from the West, whom he would command and call the Rough Riders. For some reason he felt that using these men in Cuba would overwhelm the Spanish enemy as if they had never seen horses.

New Mexico fulfilled its quota in a matter of days. The men boarded trains in the major towns and with their horses were shipped off to Florida to organize for the invasion of Cuba. Roosevelt did lead his men in the famous charge up San Juan Hill, but the Rough Riders who followed him were on foot. Their horses never left Florida.

Nonetheless, many Hispanic New Mexicans joined Roosevelt's ranks to demonstrate their patriotism. In some cases the outward affection for the United States extended beyond volunteering, and few examples could surpass one young man who served as an officer, whose very name expressed his family's sentiment. His name was George Washington Armijo. After the war, Armijo would become a local community leader as well as the person who regularly portrayed don Diego de Vargas in Santa Fe's fiestas.

∞

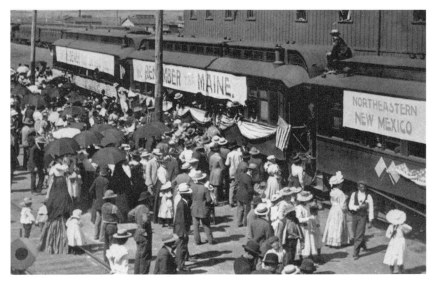

Rough Riders leaving Las Vegas, 1898. Photograph by Charles Dell. Courtesy Palace of the Governors (MNM/DCA 66657).

The national movement toward Progressivism peaked after the turn of the century and had its roots in the Populist movement led by William Jennings Bryan. Populism originated in the West and advocated against eastern banks and investors while promoting the silver monetary standard over gold. The movement gained momentum as Bryan ran for the presidency in 1896. One of Bryan's speechwriters, L. Frank Baum, wrote a political parody of the movement that he titled *The Wizard of Oz*. Oz, of course, was Washington, D.C., and the wizard was the weak president of the United States. Dorothy, the hero, came from a farm in Kansas and, in the book, wore silver shoes while she walked over the gold brick road. This represented the movement's advocacy of the silver standard over gold for the national currency.

In New Mexico the silver standard was less of an issue, but the Populist movement resonated with some of its people, for it provided an outlet for locals to express their opposition to entrenched politicians, big landowners, and the cattle kings who were fencing in the land. Fencing property was an alien concept to New Mexico's Hispanic

William Howard Taft, president of the United States, at the Alvarado Hotel in Albuquerque, 1909. From Marc Simmons, Albuquerque: A Narrative History *(Albuquerque: University of New Mexico Press, 1982). Original in the NM State Records Center and Archives.*

and Indian peoples. No wonder, then, that the Gorras Blancas rode to cut fences. No wonder, too, that the same people joined the Populist movement. They actually elected members to the territorial legislature and, for a while, posed a real threat to the established parties. The outbreak of war and Bryan's defeat pretty much ended the movement. The sentiment, however, never died.

Teddy Roosevelt parlayed his swashbuckling image into a successful political career. Upon the assassination of President William McKinley, Roosevelt became president of the United States. He never forgot New Mexico, for he attended a series of annual Rough Rider reunions in Las Vegas. Statehood appeared eminent because Roosevelt promised his men that he supported the move. Unfortunately, Roosevelt's progressive agenda never included the actuality of statehood for New Mexico. That reality was left to his "conservative" successor, William Howard Taft, who took one trip to New Mexico and then supported the legislation granting statehood. On 6 January 1912, President Taft signed the statehood proclamation and New Mexico became the forty-seventh state of the Union. Arizona, at first a part of the Territory of New Mexico and then its own territory after 1863, became the forty-eighth state over a month later, on 14 February. The honeymoon had ended and the marriage had been consummated.

Columbus, NM, in ashes after the raid of Pancho Villa's men,
March 1916. Photograph by W. H. Horne Co.
Courtesy Palace of the Governors (MNM/DCA 5805).

CHAPTER EIGHT

Statehood

THE LEGACY
CONTINUES

ᏸᎯ

New Mexico's relatively short history as a state has been anything but dull. New Mexico's prompt involvement in national as well as international events can nowhere be better illustrated then with the episode of Pancho Villa's raid on Columbus, a small village in southern New Mexico, and with the election of Octaviano Larrazolo as governor of New Mexico.

On 9 March 1916, just four years after New Mexico became a state, the federal government and probably some local profiteers and adventurers drew the state into the Mexican Revolution, which had been raging for some time. For reasons still unclear, the men of Pancho Villa, one of the main characters in the revolution, crossed the international border and entered New Mexico to surprise a small United States Army contingent stationed at Columbus. They burned down most of the town. During the fighting ten civilians and eight United States soldiers were

killed. The Villistas suffered around 170 dead, over a fourth of their force. Some of the captured Villistas were hanged before Governor Larrazolo pardoned the rest.

The reasons given for the raid range from some business deals gone bad with the Ravel Brothers Store to Villa's irritation with the United States for allowing opposition forces to be transported on U.S. railroads. The store was singled out during the hostilities, and one of the railroad branches used by Mexican forces ran through Columbus. Villa may also have wanted to demonstrate his contempt for the United States' policy relative to Germany's role in the Mexican Revolution. By this time, too, Germany was deeply involved in World War I, which was then raging in Europe.

Whatever the reason for the attack, the East Coast newspapers proclaimed in boldfaced headlines that the United States had been "invaded." The government immediately mobilized its army under the command of General John J. "Blackjack" Pershing. The military mobilization along the Mexican border was unlike any seen before, for the hardware included heretofore-untried airplanes, tanks, cars, machine guns, and gas. All of these were new innovations that were tested while locating and pursuing Pancho Villa. George Patton, one of Pershing's young second lieutenants, was the recent West Point graduate who would become frustrated with his border assignment. Patton could

The Duck Queen in Wagon Mound, ca. 1916. Courtesy Tresa Vorenberg, Santa Fe, and Palace of the Governors (MNM/DCA HP.05.12).

not understand why Villa and his cohorts would disappear into the desert and not face their enemy. With no combat experience to speak of, Patton was left to complain about the boring duty in the blowing sands of the southwestern desert.

On the face of it the United States' reaction to the raid on Columbus seemed a bit overdone. While the immediate goal was to exact revenge on Pancho Villa, the more beneficial purpose was to prepare the army with its new equipment for a much larger and more dangerous conflict. The army's experience on the border became essential to its eventual success after the United States entered World War I a year later in April of 1917.

The military exercise also hinted at another role that New Mexico would play for the United States government. New Mexico's great expanses, low population density, and great distances between population centers proved ideal for the eventual location of many military bases in the area. Combating hostile Indians gave rise to the first round of U.S. bases in the nineteenth century. Now the modern military needed space to practice and test its new weapons systems. This began with the border activities under Pershing and would continue to a crescendo during and after World War II, with the establishment of government laboratories and air force bases.

Robert Hutchings Goddard

There is a story that when World War II ended the United States
government began an inquiry about the development of Germany's
v-2 rockets, which had terrorized London. When questioned, one
German scientist reputedly replied that the United States needed
to pay more attention to Robert Goddard.

Dr. Robert Hutchings Goddard was born in Worcester,
Massachusetts, in 1882. He attended Worcester Polytechnic, where
he later taught physics while working on his master's and doctorate
degrees from Clark University. After graduating, he initially worked
as a research fellow at Princeton University in 1912, and then in 1914,
he accepted a job at his alma mater, where he would be a professor
of physics for the next twenty-nine years.

Goddard had a genius, an intellectual strength that he combined
with a shy gentleness and firm sense of mission. Many people saw
him as a personification of the mad genius, but others, like Charles
Lindbergh, Harry F. Guggenheim, and his college president, Wallace
Atwood, recognized him as a visionary genius. They were correct,
for he became a pioneering scientist.

As early as age seventeen, and before the turn of the century,
Goddard spoke and wrote about upper atmosphere space travel.
He would pursue that idea for the rest of his life, becoming, as some
have described, the man who made the greatest contribution to the
development of rockets and space travel.

His early research concentrated on rocketry even before the first
airplane! In 1908 he conducted static tests of solid-fuel rockets.
Then he developed the idea of using liquid hydrogen and oxygen
for multistage interplanetary rockets. When he joined the faculty
at Clark University, he began experimenting with larger rockets.
Here he began investigations into liquid propellant rockets, but was
interrupted by the first World War.

During the war he worked on and developed several types of
solid propellant rockets for defense against the newly developed tanks
then being used. As a result, he perfected the bazooka, which became
an integral weapon in World War II.

Goddard continued his rocket work after the war. In 1926, at

Auburn, Massachusetts, he conducted a career-changing test when he launched his first successful liquid-fuel rocket. This was the first rocket flight to carry on-board instruments. The rocket carried a barometer, thermometer, and a camera to photograph the other two instruments. The eleven-foot, six-inch rocket rose vertically to ninety feet and then traveled a horizontal distance of one hundred feet. Fortunately, no one was hurt. Nor was anyone's property damaged. But the potential for such accidents plus the subsequent publicity surrounding that test convinced Goddard, if not the local authorities, that he needed to relocate to a place where he could conduct his tests safely.

Thus, with the funding of the Daniel and Florence Guggenheim Foundation, he moved to Roswell, New Mexico. There, in the open spaces of eastern New Mexico, Dr. Goddard worked in a small laboratory outside of town, where his production was astounding. For the next decade and a half, Dr. Goddard worked and produced. He fired a rocket that traveled faster than the speed of sound. He developed push-button launches that started a process of devices that operated before the launch. He is credited with devising deflector vanes to stabilize and guide the rocket. He was the first person to demonstrate that rockets will function in a vacuum. Among his many other ideas, such as self-cooling rocket motors and landing devices, he forecast jet-driven airplanes and travel in space.

When World War II broke out, Dr. Goddard moved to Annapolis to work for the navy. He worked on a number of special projects, probably the most important of which was his work on jet-assisted takeoff devices for aircraft. He died in Annapolis on 10 August 1945 before he completed his work. But Dr. Goddard would never have finished his work.

Since his death, this mild scientist has received many honors. Scholarships and awards as well as buildings and libraries are named for him. His laboratory, tools, and several pieces of his equipment are permanently preserved in the Robert H. Goddard Planetarium of the Roswell Museum and Art Center in Roswell. There the visitor can view a permanent exhibition about him.

He was a man whose genius continues to benefit all mankind. No longer considered weird for his ideas, he became a significant part of New Mexico's scientific legacy.

Of all the government laboratories and research projects, the most famous was the secret Manhattan Project at Los Alamos that developed and tested the atom bomb, the first of which was exploded at the Trinity Site on 16 July 1945. The project's head scientist was J. Robert Oppenheimer, who had become familiar with Los Alamos while on camping vacations in the Jémez Mountains. He chose the 7,500-foot location to establish the laboratories of present-day Los Alamos. Upon seeing the power unleashed at that first explosion he quoted the Bhagavad Gita, "I am become death, the destroyer of worlds." That test firing resulted in the bombings of Hiroshima and Nagasaki, which in turn resulted in Japan's surrender from the war.

New Mexico had some particular historical connections with World War II beyond the Manhattan Project. New Mexico, like all states, sent its young off to the war. New Mexicans served in all the military branches. Some Hispanic families had as many as five or six siblings enlisted in military service. New Mexico's National Guard had been activated and sent to the Philippine Islands before the outbreak of war. There they were underfed, given inadequate supplies, and suffered the humiliation of obeying General Douglas MacArthur's order to surrender to the Japanese forces. Over ten thousand U.S. soldiers, including nearly two thousand men from the 200th and 515th Coast Artillery of New Mexico's National Guard, were taken prisoner and underwent the horrendous ordeal of being force-marched across the Bataan Peninsula to prisoner-of-war camps. There the mistreatment continued until the Japanese transported them on overcrowded ships to forced-labor camps in Japan. By the end of the war only half of the men survived to give witness to their inhumane treatment.

Navajo Indians from New Mexico and Arizona formed the now famous "code talkers." These Navajo volunteers in the Marine Corps sent coded messages in their native language throughout the South Pacific. The Japanese could not break the code because it could not translate the Navajo language. The U.S. command in the South Pacific theater could discuss and set strategy without fear of the enemy deciphering what they were saying.

Ernie Pyle, one of the war's major correspondents, heralded from Albuquerque, where he worked as a journalist. He gave up his job to join the U.S. forces as they island-hopped across the South Pacific. He chose

Funeral in the Santa Fe Japanese Internment Camp. An elderly man passed away and his son was recalled from U.S. military service to attend the funeral, ca. 1945. Photograph courtesy Joe Ando.

to be at the front to share the experiences of those in harm's way. There, at the small island of Ie Shima, west of Okinawa, a sniper's bullet killed the man whose words still live. The popular movie *G.I. Joe* featured Pyle.

Another famous journalist, Bill Mauldin, came from Alamogordo. He served in the European theater. Mauldin's cartoons of G.I. Joe and his buddy, Willie, once again championed the plight of the common soldier. The sometimes sarcastic bite of Mauldin's work even caused the wrath of General George Patton, who, as noted above, had begun his career in the southern New Mexico not far from where Mauldin spent his youth.

As the United States waged war abroad, the government as well as society moved into a wartime mode at home. New Mexico became involved in one of the government's more infamous projects, the removal of Japanese people from the West Coast to internment camps. Santa Fe became the location of a Department of Justice camp, where some 4,500 men, most of them elderly, were held over a four-year period. Deming, Alamogordo, and Lordsburg became designated locations for holding German prisoners of war. The vestiges of the German camps remain in New Mexico today.

∞

The Very Large Array in search of knowledge. From Karen Taschek,
Death Stars, Weird Galaxies, and a Quasar-Spangled Universe:
The Discoveries of the Very Large Array Telescope *(Albuquerque:*
University of New Mexico Press, 2006). Photograph courtesy
National Radio Astronomy Observatory.

United States government expenditures continued in New Mexico
after the Second World War. The laboratories in Los Alamos continued their contracted research. Sandia Laboratories and White Sands
Missile Range brought more scientists to a state already boasting of a
plethora of novelists, historians, archaeologists, and artists. Various air
force bases took advantage of New Mexico's open spaces and in turn
gave economic boosts to places like Albuquerque, Alamogordo,
Roswell, and Portales. Even when Roswell's air base closed, the people
were able to maintain their town to such an extent that it was named
one of America's most livable cities. However, most of the bases and
research laboratories are still an important part of New Mexico's economic mix. On a per capita basis, New Mexico gets as much federal
money as any state.

The search for knowledge, begun by those researchers at the end of
the nineteenth century, was extended into the science of the twentieth

*Ralph Emerson
Twitchell, historian,
ca. 1910. Photograph
courtesy Palace of the
Governors
(MNM/DCA 7902).*

century. In 1981, the Very Large Array, a futuristic radio telescope, was installed over thirteen miles across the Plains of San Agustin west of Socorro. The second space shuttle to be launched landed at White Sands.

∞

As the federal government poured money into New Mexico for research in weapons, flight, and space, the arts and humanities had its own renaissance. There was a turn-of-the-century confluence of creative minds and interest in history and archaeology that began in the territorial years and germinated in the early statehood years. Ralph E. Twitchell became to New Mexico history what Bandelier is to southwestern archaeology. He was the first person to systematically use the Spanish and Mexican

Ernest Thompson Seton

Ernest Thompson Seton was born in England in 1860 as Ernest Evan Thompson. Before he died in Santa Fe in 1946 he would become one of the United States' greatest and most unheralded naturalists. He painted and illustrated and wrote novels about nature. His relative anonymity is partially attributed to World War I, which broke out at the peak of his career, and World War II, which lasted until a year before his death.

He was born into a wealthy family that lost its fortune when he was five years old. As a result the family moved to Canada, where he grew up. He returned to England to attend the London Academy of Art before moving to western Canada. He then moved to New York City in his early twenties, and there he began his career.

Between trips to Paris, where he attended art schools, he returned to Canada, where he became known for his sketches in *Center Magazine*. While in New York he met a rancher from Clayton, New Mexico, and became intrigued enough about the place. He went there early in the 1920s. While in Clayton he became fascinated with wolves and began writing short stories about a wolf he named Lobo (Spanish for "wolf") and its female companion, which he named Blanca (Spanish for "white"). He originally published the stories in magazines, but their popularity soon dictated that they be published as books. His books became very popular and with the help of some wise investments Seton became a wealthy man.

archives as well as more current data in English to write and publish histories of New Mexico. All subsequent historians of New Mexico owe a debt to his work.

Art and artists became a major contributing economic factor in the state. New Mexico's vast expanses, scenery, and seemingly exotic peoples attracted artists of all kinds. The art trend began in the nineteenth century with the likes of Lachlan Allan MacLean, who was a soldier with the U.S. Army during the Mexican War, and Richard Kern, whose illustrations possibly include the earliest depiction of the Palace of the Governors. The trend continued with people like Leon Trousset, a Frenchman who traveled through the area painting the plazas of the towns, and Charles Lummis, whose camera recorded images that would

His first wife was wealthy as well. She was also artistically inclined and helped design his books. At the time, the success of his writing overwhelmed his own art, as he wrote an astounding seventy-five books. All his work, whether in writing or in art, dealt with nature and its inherent beauty.

He traveled throughout his life. He formed the Woodcraft League in Connecticut in an effort to draw youth into an early appreciation of the natural world. His organization became one of the precursors to the Boy Scouts of America. Lord Baden Powell in England organized a similar but more militaristic organization that became the Boy Scouts of England, an organization that also was a precursor to the Boy Scouts of America. Their creator's work in the two organizations and their eventual evolution into the Boy Scouts of America have been a source of debate ever since. Suffice it to say that the Boy Scouts of America's great mountain ranch, The Philmont, outside of Cimarron, New Mexico, has on its grounds the Ernest Thompson Seton Museum, with much of his art and collections that give evidence of the serious and meticulous effort he exerted.

After 1930 Seton moved to Santa Fe, where he lived until his death. His house south of town became legendary for its distinct architectural style as well as the constant gathering of other intelligent and artistic people. Often referred to as Seton Village or Seton Castle, the home was but a small reminder of the preponderance of his work and influence.

attract others. By the twentieth century the seeds had been sown. New Mexico had become a real destination for creative and talented minds. Possibly inspired by the images of earlier artists and the publicity of the railroads, these men and women sought an environment that would stimulate them. Because of them, New Mexico became famous for its art. Building on traditions begun in the Native American and Hispanic communities, along with those of the artists of the territorial years, New Mexico became known as an "art colony" during the statehood period.

The railroads, especially the AT&SF, created national campaigns to attract people to the Southwest. The AT&SF and its related Harvey House Hotels became a major promoter of the area. The Harvey Girls guided tours to various scheduled Indian dances or to natural and historical sites. Tourists, no doubt influenced by the railroads and the influx of photographers like W. H. Jackson and Charles Lummis, among others, traveled to the "exotic" West. Illustrations and descriptions of the Southwest became popular in East Coast publications. These, in turn, inspired still more artists, photographers, and writers to travel west and record their impressions.

In 1912, Taos became a focal point for some of those artists. Bert Phillips and Ernest Blumenschein, who first traveled to Taos in 1898, decided to make the northern New Mexico village their home. They were quickly joined by a number of other, now legendary, artists and they formed the Taos Society of Artists to promote their work.

The devastation of World War I and the subsequent period called the "Roaring Twenties," a kind of national, live-for-today holiday, gave rise to an increased influx of "sensitive minds" to New Mexico. Many creative people felt that the United States had become decadent and that Europe, despite the tragedy of the recent war, still had a sense of time and history. So many left the United States to go to Europe. This was almost a reversal of what the Pilgrims and Puritans had believed when they migrated to America. Writers like Henry James and F. Scott Fitzgerald are two examples of these ex-patriot free thinkers.

Others found in New Mexico a poor man's Europe that served the same purpose. Some, like Mabel Dodge Luhan and Eugenie Shonnard, went to Europe then ended up in New Mexico. Even Europeans like D. H. Lawrence and Leon Gaspard found their ideal creative environment in New Mexico. New Mexico's natural beauty plus its "foreign" local populations, tolerance, and sense of timelessness appealed to these creative people.

Within a couple of decades these "bohemians," as the locals called them, not only created a major art colony in New Mexico but they also discovered the artistic traditions that New Mexicans had been pursuing for centuries. The creation of the Museum of New Mexico, with its various museums; the School of American Research; the Spanish Colonial Art Society, with its Spanish markets; and the Annual Indian Market, now run by the Southwest Indian Association, are all attributable to this renaissance.

Today, tourism is a major New Mexican industry. Indeed, it may be New Mexico's most important as well as most lucrative industry. More money is spent for art in the state's capital than in any United States city outside of New York and Los Angeles. The fact that New Mexico has more scientists, published authors, and artists per capita than any other state in the Union is a phenomenon born out of its history.

∞

Governor Larrazolo, who was born in Mexico, is illustrative of New Mexico's political history. Like many states, New Mexico has its cast of colorful political leaders. Interestingly enough, some centuries-old trends have been maintained as a part of New Mexico's political patrimony. For example, by the time of statehood some ninety-three individuals had been appointed governor under the administrations of Spain, Mexico, and the United States. Of these, only a handful were born in New Mexico. The percentage of native New Mexicans elected governor during the statehood period has improved only slightly. Specifically, out of a total of twenty-six New Mexican governors who have taken office since 1912, only eight were born in the state or territory.

The Hispanic community has always maintained a political influence at the local as well as state levels. Octaviano Larrazolo, Dennis Chávez, and Joseph Montoya all became United States Senators. New Mexico has sent six Hispanics to serve as United States Congressmen.

A generation of young Hispanic New Mexicans returned from World War II and took advantage of the G.I. Bill to receive college educations, the influence of which has yet to be thoroughly studied. As veterans who traveled throughout the world, met different people, and returned home proud of their service, they developed different attitudes about their place in society. They saw themselves as full members of the United States, having demonstrated their loyalty. One manifestation of this ideal was to erase any reason for past wrongs, and that included making sure that their children did not grow up handicapped by speaking English with a Spanish accent. Thus a good number of Hispanic baby boomers were intentionally brought up speaking only English. The irony is that most of their parents were bilingual and spoke without accents.

The powerful role of Hispanics in the legislature as well as in the local communities that were established under Spanish or Mexican rule continues. However, the political representation has also reflected changes in the populace as a whole. Today, an influx of retired people as well as people looking for jobs is slowly changing the demography, if not lifestyles, of the area. In some respects, these two groups represent opposite extremes, because many of the retired move to the state with good incomes, while an increasing percentage of the job hunters have migrated from poverty in other countries, especially Mexico.

∞

As mentioned, New Mexico greatly benefited from federal expenditures. This is largely attributable to Clyde Tingley, who was Albuquerque's city manager and then governor of New Mexico. With the help of U.S. Senators Carl Hatch and Dennis Chávez, Tingley befriended President Franklin Roosevelt. The resulting infusion of federal programs, such as the WPA (Works Progress Administration), created jobs across the state's economic spectrum, thus softening the effects of the Great Depression. New roads, buildings, schools, and infrastructure, such as dams creating electricity and sewer systems, changed New Mexico. The same government monies paid artists and writers to create public art and record oral histories. The National Historic Buildings Surveys recorded detailed drawings of the state's many historic structures and town plans.

An important effect of the Depression in New Mexico was the influx of "Okies," those people from the southern plains who, because of the Depression and drought, were forced to leave their homes to survive elsewhere. Many traveled through New Mexico on their way to the promise of the West Coast. The image of these people with all their possessions tied to their cars and trucks is still vivid among many New Mexicans today. Many local households fed these migrants as they passed through the state. These people met different fates and some were exploited. Some were arrested as vagrants and, without trial, forced to work on "road gangs." Others chose to remain in New Mexico to become a part of a society already very inclusive.

∞

Railroad and mines in Madrid, ca. 1919. Photograph by T. Harmon Parkhurst. Courtesy Palace of the Governors (MNM/DCA 5226).

The mining industry continued to grow throughout World War II. Extractive resources became increasingly important for the war effort. Coal, copper, and uranium became priorities. Large companies recruited local labor, as well as some workers from Mexico. In the 1920s, a de facto *bracero* program, initiated under President Venustiano Carranza, allowed Mexican workers to come to the United States legally. In 1942, the United States signed the Bracero Treaty to help fill a depleted labor market that was being diverted to the war effort.

A good portion of the mining labor force came from countries other than the United States. Italians prevailed in the Raton area, while Mexicans concentrated in western New Mexico. These workers together with the local labor supply of Native Americans, New Mexican Hispanics, and others amounted to a very diverse labor force. In some cases, the diversity worked. Such an example would be the coal mining enterprise in Madrid, a company town whose sense of community was expressed through its semi-pro baseball team and its Christmas displays.

For all of the miners, however, the work was dangerous and hard. Industrial accidents, pollution, and labor strife became a part of New Mexican life. Workers were usually employed by companies that had no local connections. Mining disasters such as those in 1913 and again in 1923 near Raton, in the community of Dawson, brought overwhelming grief to whole communities. Racial tensions were a part of the bitter strikes and violence that occurred at Gallup and Silver City. The story of the last strike, in which wives of the miners risked their lives to man the strike lines, is told in a controversial film called *Salt of the Earth*, which has become a cult classic.

∞

The end of World War II brought on the cold war on the national level. New Mexico's labor disputes and *Salt of the Earth*–type manifestos naturally enough were connected to accusations of disloyalty as the country went through a kind of patriotic paranoia most vividly illustrated by McCarthyism. At the same time, the country prospered and New Mexico benefited as well. New Mexico has changed more in the last sixty years than it has at any other time in its history. Population increased at rapid rates as more people moved in for health and retirement. Others took up residence on a time-share basis to enjoy the land's enchantment. And the state developed new attractions.

The ski industry developed with the construction of internationally known resorts at Taos, Santa Fe, Red River, and Cloudcroft, along with many smaller ski areas. The state and national park systems both developed so that today almost half of the state's land is preserved for the enjoyment of many future generations of people. Fishing, hunting, hiking, and camping at the state's many parks have become a major attraction. Federal parks and monuments such as Carlsbad Caverns, White Sands, the Pecos Pueblo ruins, Bandelier, and Chaco Canyon complement a state park system of monuments, including the town of Lincoln, Fort Seldon, and the Jémez Mission ruins, among others. These monuments and parks attract millions of visitors annually.

The state's many museums continue to be an attraction. Today the state operates museums in Santa Fe, Albuquerque, Las Cruces, and Alamogordo. The museums, along with the monuments and parks, reflect the growth and economic importance of New Mexico's cultural tourism, which the state has nourished. By the end of the twentieth century, New Mexico's government provided more money for art and culture per capita than any other state in the country. And private institutions followed suit. Music, in the form of the Santa Fe Opera and Chamber Music Festival, the Southwest Opera, the New Mexico Symphony Orchestra, plus orchestras in Santa Fe, Roswell, Los Alamos, and Las Cruces, to name a few, and local museums in almost every town make New Mexico a cultural treasure trove.

The result was inevitable. New Mexico was "discovered," first with Santa Fe. The "city different," as it called itself, became a destination, and its discovery was followed, in quick succession, by that of Taos, Ruidoso, Silver City, and now Albuquerque and Las Cruces.

Roswell, in eastern New Mexico, lost its military base, developed the New Mexico Military Institute, and started businesses that train commercial airline pilots at its abandoned air base and built buses, to become "a model city." In addition, a mysterious post–World War II event has turned Roswell into the focal point for believers of extraterrestrial visitors. Its UFO museum is one of the most popular in the state.

New Mexico's Indian communities asserted rights that were won in the courts to prohibit non-Indian visits to sacred areas and functions, while encouraging attendance at open ceremonials. Indian communities have also constructed resorts for golf, hunting, and fishing, which have been an economic boon for both the tribes and the state. More recently, the proliferation of Indian casinos has been a Native American attempt to seek new sources of revenue. More importantly, the casinos have become a benchmark of the various tribes' determination to be self-reliant.

Native American art forms, first promoted by the railroads and then by the Museum of New Mexico, Santa Fe's Indian Market in the 1920s, along with the nation's largest powwow at Gallup, have flourished. Indian art is in constant jeopardy, though, as mass-produced non-Indian-made copies continue to be sold. Such fake art undersells the handmade works. The popularity of Indian art, as well as antiquities, has given rise to another problem. The insidious practice of pothunting consists of arbitrarily and illegally digging up invaluable sites to find old pots and other artifacts that are then sold

Norman Petty

Norman Petty needs a statue. Born and educated in Clovis, New Mexico, where he directed his school's band, he would go on to make history. Still, Petty is an unsung personage when compared to the many better-known people whom he helped achieve fame.

Petty was born in 1927 and died in 1984. He spent his whole life in and around his hometown. He loved music and by the 1950s was a professional musician. He liked popular, rock and roll and named his first group The Torchy Swingsters. He was good enough in his youth to score the famous Duke Ellington song "Mood Indigo."

In 1954, Petty decided to make music in a different way. Rather than be up front playing it, he decided to work behind the scenes creating it. He purchased his uncle's vacant store, which was located next to his parents' filling station. There he built and installed a state-of-the-art recording studio and within two years he would make rock and roll history.

Petty did more than record. He arranged and produced. He clearly became a major influence on his industry and nothing could be more illustrative than his relationship with Buddy Holly.

Holly traveled to Petty's studio after a bad experience trying to record in Nashville. After three sessions in Tennessee he was judged "the biggest no talent I ever worked with." Yet, with Petty, Buddy Holly became a nationwide household name.

On their first night working together they recorded two songs, "I'm Looking for Someone to Love" and "That'll Be the Day." In the

for profit. State and National Preservation Acts, along with various government offices, help combat such activities, but it has been a constant struggle.

The last third of the twentieth century has seen a resurgence in Spanish language and culture. Some examples of this change are the increase in membership in the Penitente confraternities, a plethora of New Mexican Hispanic writers, and the astounding popularity of the Spanish Market, which has expanded to include both traditional and nontraditional arts. Mirroring the inception of Indian art and culture museums and the Indian Pueblo Cultural Center in Albuquerque, next fifteen months, Holly and his band, The Crickets, recorded sixteen more rock and roll classics. In the process, they created the "Clovis sound." John Lennon later claimed that the Beatles' first forty songs consciously tried to recreate the Clovis sound as they mimicked Buddy Holly. The Rolling Stones' first hit single was a cover of Holly's "Rave On." Paul McCartney, Lennon's longtime partner, eventually purchased the publishing rights to all of Holly's songs.

Norman Petty, who was the genius behind Holly, launched many careers in Clovis. Petty influenced Roy Orbison, Waylon Jennings, and a lesser-known group from Raton, New Mexico, called The Fireballs. The Fireballs are known for their still-popular song "Sugar Shack," which they recorded with Petty. Petty's own group, The Roses, which he used in the studio, has been inducted into the Hall of Fame in Nashville.

Norman Petty clearly influenced rock and roll. He was a forceful man who did not hesitate to make a suggestion. Nevertheless, he recognized talent and allowed talented musicians to express their individual genius. He encouraged experimentation. He intentionally created a "hothouse" environment to nourish and produce the result of the collective energy of those involved with the sessions. An example of this is having the drummer play an empty box that sat on his knees. This technique was used in Holly's songs "Not Fade Away" and "Every Day." Petty also suggested the use of a miniature xylophone in Holly's "Every Day."

Today, Lubbock, Texas, just across the border from Clovis, honors its native son Buddy Holly with a prominent statue. Such an honor for the man who made Holly is long overdue in New Mexico.

Hispanic-focused museums such as the Millicent Rogers Museum in Taos, El Rancho de las Golondrinas, the private Museum of Spanish Colonial Arts, and the National Hispanic Cultural Center have become popular disseminators and promoters of Hispanic culture. These institutions reflect the growing pride as well as influence of New Mexico's Hispanic community.

Nevertheless, old conflicts and struggles persist. Traditional land-ownership and water rights continue to be a source of contention in the state's courts. Old methods and celebrations sometimes come into conflict with modern society. People growing up in rural communities

Mystery in Roswell

A newspaperman following up on a story, a betrothed nurse who disappeared, and something that fell out of the sky. These are part of a story that has not been resolved.

On the evening of 2 July 1947, William "Mac" Brazel, a rancher, was in his ranch house on his lands some seventy-five miles northwest of Roswell and a little south of Corona, New Mexico. In the midst of a severe lightning storm, he heard a loud explosion. The next day he discovered a crash site. What he saw and collected would begin a tale of an unexplained incident of something falling out of the sky and crashing. Others witnessed the object hitting or exploding at Brazel's ranch and coming to rest at Magdalena Flats, west of Socorro, where a team of archaeologists as well as a civil engineer in soil conservation working for the federal government also saw the wreckage.

The United States Army and its affiliated Air Corps, which that very year was being reorganized into a separate branch of the military, took an immediate interest in both sites. They closed the sites, swore everyone to secrecy, collected all the wreckage, and immediately shipped it out of state.

There also seems to have been some fatalities associated with the wreck. Some people claimed to have seen short, semihumanoid figures with oversize heads and slanted eyes, but this part of the story is hazy.

Mac Brazel, shaken by his discovery, talked to a neighbor and then went to the local sheriff. He eventually gave an interview and shared his story, albeit reluctantly, to others. He was interrogated by the army when he took them to the site. News of his discovery soon spread. The Roswell Air Base actually released a statement that they had "gained possession" of a "flying disc" from an extraterrestrial crash. The local newspaper editor, who knew the sheriff, secured enough information to confirm the base's press release. On 8 July he published the story under the headline, "RAAF Captures Flying Saucer on Ranch in Roswell Region." The local radio station contacted its sister station, KOB, in Albuquerque and began teletyping the story. The teletype went dead, but not before the amazing story got out on the wires.

Almost immediately, attempts were made to stop the news. The army reversed its story, shipped its public relations officer out of Roswell, and announced that the collected material was nothing but a weather balloon. Many people, including the federal government itself, have since refuted this explanation.

The newspaper received telephone calls from Washington, D.C., ordering it to stop printing stories about flying saucers. This, they were told, was a matter of security. Obviously the newspaper's employees were intimidated. But their curiosity was tweaked as well. They learned that the local funeral home had received an inquiry from the base asking how many child-sized caskets they had in stock. And, when a reporter and friend went to the hospital to follow up, they were met by the friend's fiancée, who worked there as a nurse. Obviously preoccupied, she very seriously told them that they "did not want to know" what was in the hospital and that they should leave. Within a week they were informed that she had "moved to England" and her betrothed in Roswell never heard from her again.

The radio station manager feared that he would have problems with the FCC when he was told to stop following the story. The manager in Albuquerque recalls that nobody would talk about the incident. Once again national security came up. Even United States Senator Dennis Chávez telephoned the station about cooperating with the federal authorities.

So what happened? The United States Army, the Pentagon, and the United States government never have given a viable explanation outside of the refuted balloon story. The many witnesses, the people transferred away, and imposed secrecy has only conspired to grow the "Roswell Incident," now the title of a book, and make Roswell the UFO capitol of the United States. Today, Roswell's International UFO Museum and Research Center is one of the most visited museums in the state and the annual UFO celebration attracts tens of thousands of believers. Two of the three founders of the Museum and Research Center were Walter Haut and Glenn Dennis. The former was the decorated lieutenant public information officer who first released the story, and the latter worked at the funeral home that was involved in the mystery. Whatever it was that crashed in 1947 remains a government secret.

The Spanish Market, Santa Fe, ca. 1990. Photograph by Gene Peach. Courtesy Museum of Spanish Colonial Art.

are suddenly encountering urban growth. They cannot keep their livestock, even if it only amounts to a pig and some chickens. And shopping malls or major discount stores are built on the seemingly abundant land.

The Philmont Boy Scout Ranch by Cimarron; the Santa Fe Opera; Ruidoso's horseracing track, where, for years, the richest race in the country was run; Albuquerque's International Balloon Fiesta; and the rebirth and success of a wine-producing industry all speak to the diverse vibrancy of activity in New Mexico. Transportation at the beginning of the twentieth century was horses and trains. The car and truck replaced the horse and wagon, but trains continue to transport goods and people. And as this book is published, state and federal leaders have come to realize the importance of improved local train transportation. The automobile gave rise to paved roads and highways, extensive parking lots, malls, the rise and fall of drive-in theaters, and the fall and rise of downtowns. Albuquerque, ideally situated in the center of the state, became a transportation hub for ground travel, and then air travel with its international airport. All this modernity, perhaps most symbolized by the national laboratories at Los Alamos and Sandia or the giant Intel installation at Rio Rancho, has speeded up New Mexico's traditional lifestyle.

Water, or more specifically, water preservation, has become a New Mexican priority. Dams on the Chama, Rio Grande, and Pecos rivers, along with water diversion projects, have struggled to keep enough water to supply a population that more than doubled in the last half century. Las Cruces has surpassed Santa Fe as the state's second-largest city. Albuquerque, the state's largest city, has expanded to the point where in the next few years, more people will be living on the west side of the river than the east side, where the city began and became modern.

Santa Fe in many ways has become symbolic of New Mexico. The capital city is a tourist center as well as a faddish place. Because of an influx of higher-income people, Santa Fe has become the state's most expensive place to live by far. This has resulted in criticism from long-time locals who feel that all the attention to development has negatively impacted their lifestyle and has driven up the cost of living beyond their incomes.

While the seventies, eighties, and early nineties saw a decrease in the percentage of Hispanic-surnamed inhabitants in Santa Fe as well as statewide, by the end of the century there was a sudden increase in that segment of the population. The Hispanic population is projected to once again be a majority in New Mexico within the next decade.

Thus, the state that many people in the United States still do not recognize as a part of the country; the only state in the Union with "USA" on its license plates; and the state still considered economically poor by some standards, has become a desirable place to live and a destination to visit. But, it is a place with a message for the future.

"Mi macho moro y un coyote que cogi" (*My brave white horse and a coyote that I caught*). *Mariano Chávez in Carrizo Canyon near Roy, NM. October 3, 1917. Mariano Chávez Collection, Fray Angélico Chávez Library. Photograph courtesy Palace of the Governors (MNM/DCA 153421).*

The Virgin and the Dynamo

Cultures, Technology, and Survival— New Mexico's Message of Enchantment

꧁꧂

History has never been entertainment for me. It truly is a philosophy as well as a discipline. The lessons inherent in the story or stories are beneficial and can, perhaps should, help humankind constantly improve upon the decisions of previous generations. Like a physics problem that appears to continue into infinity, history as a discipline first needs to be recorded as objectively as humanly possible, and then improved as it progresses through generations and time.

But a foible is the problem of an error's effect over time. If a person begins a trip one degree off center, the journey will progressively move farther and farther from the intended path the farther that person travels. So history as a philosophy must identify those true lessons, correct misdirection, and apply to the present, for the future, the heritage left in yesteryear's experience.

New Mexico's history is a case study of a landlocked land where, through the centuries, various peoples settled. They never settled in preponderant numbers and perhaps that is why no group ever overwhelmed its predecessors. All the peoples who have settled in New Mexico have survived in New Mexico. These include Hohokam, Mogollon, Anasazi, Athabaskan, Spanish, Mexican, and many other groups from all parts of North America. Those people also represent a variety of religions, from the many Native American religions to Judeo-Christian, as well as today's many-faceted New Agers. All the cultures that came to New Mexico became a part of its society. So when the observer steps away from the details to view the big picture, New Mexico has a message applicable to all of humanity.

Simply put, New Mexicans know that it is all right to attend an Indian ceremonial or wear handmade Indian jewelry and not kill the dancers or artisans. They know that they can eat chile, even for breakfast, and not kill the cook. They have learned that knowledge of more than one language is enriching rather than degrading, and that the practice of different religions does not detract from any one faith.

This all sounds so simple, even basic, yet the lack of understanding of these very concepts is at the heart of many of humankind's problems. The world's most recent hot spots in Eastern Europe, Ireland, the Middle East, and the inner cities of the United States, to name a few, have degenerated into violence because people will kill the dancers, artisans, cooks, speakers, and practitioners of something different than their own.

New Mexico's history offers an alternative to this debauchery. It is a history that demonstrates the value of inclusivity versus exclusivity, or regeneration rather than degeneration. New Mexicans know and have inherited the idea that they are richer and better off because of all the cultures and people who have flourished in the state.

The narrative history as written here, and surely as noted by the reader, is by no means complete. As is usually the case, the narrative seems to be more coherent earlier in time. One of history's ironies, to me, is that the less we understand of an historical period or subject, the easier it is to narrate. The closer the researcher gets to the present, and the more information that is available, the more difficult and subjective the narration becomes. All people make history. Their very lives are histories, but for objectivity's sake others must judge the impact of their stories.

Yet, in New Mexico, history is a way of life. Its lessons are very much in the consciousness of the inhabitants. The strength of historic preservation laws and organizations is a natural outgrowth of New Mexico's cultural environment. But nuances exist. For example, some pueblos are more conservative than others, yet all of them maintain their traditions, their "autonomy." San Juan, where Oñate originally housed his settlement, has survived over four centuries of outside influence. One of New Mexico's greatest examples of syncretism, the melding of cultures, takes place every Christmas Eve at San Juan. An evening Catholic vespers is held with recitations in English and music sung in Tewa. Everything is hand-signed traditionally, while through it all the local Penitentes chant the rosary in Spanish. The ceremony morphs into a Matachines dance, performed at San Juan Pueblo, that begins in the church and continues through the village, which is lit by bonfires. The masked dancers mark time to the violins and guitars playing music from centuries past in Spain or Mexico. The dance's origins are still subject to debate among experts.

Jémez Pueblo holds an annual bull run every August. The event is a function of descendants of Pecos Pueblo people, who abandoned the defunct pueblo in 1838. Those people secured permission to move to Jémez, the only other pueblo that spoke Towa. They took with them their ceremonial icons and traditions, among which was the bull run, copied in the distant past from the Spanish. The bull is not real and the run is done in fun, although religious connotations cannot be overlooked.

The Navajo Tribe, the Diné, has a "Mexican clan" made up of descendants of people stolen in raids upon Hispanic communities, mostly along the Rio Puerco and Chama Rivers. Like the genízaros in Hispanic society, these people have become full participants in their host culture.

The vast majority of people in New Mexico live in towns with Spanish names or Spanish phonetic spellings of Native American names, such as Pojoaque, Taos, Tesuque, or the neighborhood of Analco, as mentioned earlier. English adaptations for pronunciation have resulted in oddities such as dropping the first "r" in Alburquerque or pronouncing Madrid with a long "a" rather than a short "a." Many modern maps have "Seboyeta" for the correct "Cebolleta." Even the ancient capital of Santa Fe is regularly and universally mispronounced "Saanafey." And local, educated Hispanics argue over whether or not the one-syllable word "Fe" in Santa Fe takes an accent. "Asi es Nuevo Mexico" ("that is [uniquely] New Mexico," or more loosely, "only in New Mexico") is one answer to all these historical facets.

But, how do we make sense of New Mexico's history? It is not solely about cultural conflict—the easy way to define or categorize ourselves. I believe a more practical answer lies in the words of Henry Adams, one of North America's geniuses. Adams was the great-grandson of Abigail and John Adams. John Adams was George Washington's vice president and the second president of the United States. Abigail was arguably the most intelligent woman of her time. Henry Adams's grandfather was John Quincy Adams, who served as the sixth president of the United States, and his father, Francis, ran for vice president and was appointed ambassador to Great Britain during the Civil War.

Like his famous ancestors, Henry Adams was trained to lead and to be called to service for his country. Yet, he never received the call and never worked a day in his life for the government. Instead, he studied, traveled, taught, and wrote history and literature.

Adams wrote a book titled *The Education of Henry Adams*. He wrote out of personal disappointment and attempted to explain a profound change, as he observed, in the United States. He observed the decline of leadership in the United States during the last third of the nineteenth century. Adams parroted Mark Twain's and Charles Dudley Warner's assessments that the times were "gilded," and L. Frank Baum's assertion that the Wizard of Oz was a phony and of little help. Adams wrote, "On the whole, even for Senators, diplomats, and Cabinet officers, the period was wearisome and stale."

Today, with the advantage of hindsight, historians agree that the last third of the nineteenth century was a low point in the quality of

U.S. presidents and political leadership. Adams correctly concluded the same thing.

This puzzled him and he sought an answer to this apparent decline. He found his answer and summarized it in a chapter titled "The Dynamo and the Virgin" in his book. The cathedral in Chartres, France, and the World's Columbian Exposition in Chicago, Illinois, gave him his insight. And that idea, that model, unbeknown to him, would apply to New Mexico, a place he never visited.

Upon observing the cathedral in Chartres, he noted that people built it in a time that was much simpler. They knew how to drop a plumb line to get a straight wall or how to create fire for heat and light from sparks. They did not even question the existence of an afterlife. And, as he noted, the descendants of the builders still live in the village in houses gathered around the cathedral that was built as a monument to the Virgin. It was as if symbolically, even unconsciously, the people had heeded the Virgin's theological call for unity. Like New Mexico's Conquistadora, Adams recognized the idea of the Virgin's conquest. The Virgin drew energy to herself, unified the community, and maintained a simple and comfortable order of things.

Then, at the World's Columbian Exposition, which closed in 1900, he found his foil. There, he noted a new invention that was the centerpiece of the exposition. The dynamo spun and hummed, creating electricity, which created light. This new invention spun in the middle of an exhibition hall, and Adams watched it as its humming lulled a baby to sleep. Yet he postulated that the gizmo's operation and very purpose was beyond the comprehension of the babe and its mother. It threw energy out, away from it, to create electricity. Adams saw that as symbolic of a modern society, no longer simple and comprehending, but being thrown into chaos that questioned and was confused.

To bring the analogy up to date, let us state that most people today could not create a spark, much less light. They would have even more trouble explaining how electricity creates light. Thus, by Adams's model, history has progressed from the simple to the complex. This is not unlike a latter-day model created by theoretical physicist, Nobel laureate, and Santa Fe resident Murray Gell-Mann. He used the example of his discovery of the quark—the basic building block of all atomic nuclei throughout the universe—along with the fundamental laws of physics, to create the idea that everything evolves from simplicity to complexity. He symbolized complexity with the example of the Jaguar (the complex). So history does the same, yet I am postulating the opposite, for out of its complexity is born a simple basic tenant for survival. And that is that all peoples live better in tolerance than otherwise. Echoing the early nineteenth-century views of Alexander von Humboldt, Gell-Mann wrote in his book *The Quark and the Jaguar: Adventures in the Simple and the Complex,* that

> it is worth a great effort to preserve both biological and cultural diversity. . . . Today the network of relationships linking the human race to itself and to the rest of the biosphere is so complex that all aspects affect all others to an extraordinary degree.

Therefore, Adams's title needs to be reversed, with priority given to the Virgin. The "Virgin and the Dynamo" model is about evolution in the technological age. It claims that in the last century and a half, technology has had and continues to have a more profound impact on humankind than any cultural interaction. The "Virgin and the Dynamo" poses old world/new world, preservation/progress, and traditional/nontraditional paradoxes. Within its message is the transcendental criticism of the natural, placid, beautiful valley whose very nature is being rudely violated by the steam-propelled train that is whistling and billowing smoke as it loudly travels through the valley. Adams even commented that "All the steam in the world could not, like the Virgin, build Chartres."

This is what New Mexico has become. A place where yesteryear and the future come together and the various long-surviving cultures are a part of the mix. The Virgin and the dynamo confront, adjust, and repeat the process all the while creating something different. Dr. Gell-Mann's choice of Santa Fe to establish the Santa Fe Institute for research on simplicity, complexity, and adaptive systems makes perfect sense.

So the preservation of languages, customs, and traditions sounds simple enough. But it is not so simple. Take Indian casinos, to name one example. Casinos are not traditional. Yet they are established to create revenue in a modern society so that longtime traditions can be maintained.

Windmills in New Mexico, a future source of energy.
From Roberts et al., Our New Mexico: A Twentieth Century
History *(Albuquerque: University of New Mexico Press, 2005).*
Photograph by Norman Johnson.

Many people have moved to New Mexico "to smell the roses," as the saying goes. For the most part, they have left hurried lifestyles to slow down in New Mexico. They have chosen New Mexico for many of the same reasons that motivated those early artists who moved to the area. Those people have chosen the Virgin and left the dynamo.

Then, in New Mexico, we learn that the dynamo is not the enemy. It is inanimate and many of its practitioners have learned to use it to enhance the Virgin. Modern science and technology can prolong life, care for the environment, as well as protect and disseminate knowledge, all of which benefit humanity. The dynamo is also present in New Mexico's research laboratories, hospitals, developments, dams, and so on. The key in New Mexico is the inclusivity demonstrated throughout its history. That very ideal will use the dynamo to the Virgin's advantage. The Virgin will survive.

And the varied peoples in their equally varied environments will live together through the now rapid technological changes and impacts. New Mexico's history is important, for it is a message for the rest of the world, and a history that has a value for the future of all humanity.

Selected Bibliography

✿

The bibliophile should note that the list of references is not a complete bibliography, but rather a list of books that were used as a basis for this book. In addition, it is an attempt to help the person who has just started reading about New Mexico's history. Here is a list that, if used, would probably make the reader more knowledgeable than the author of this book. Obviously, the list is subjective and many fine books are missing.

The same sentiment applies to the separate list of historical novels about or pertinent to New Mexico. Many years of working with the interested public have convinced me that a great introduction to history can be a historical novel.

Finally, the interested public many times has raised the question about historical readings for youth. This is a field that has been sparse over the years and only now has become an emphasis.

History books

Adams, Eleanor B. *Bishop Tamaron's Visitation of New Mexico, 1760*. Albuquerque: Historical Society of New Mexico, 1954.

Adams, Eleanor B., and Fray Angélico Chávez, trans and eds. *The Missions of New Mexico, 1776: A Description, with Other Contemporary Documents*. Albuquerque: University of New Mexico Press, 1956.

Alberts, Don E. *The Battle of Glorieta: Union Victory in the West.* College Station: Texas A&M University Press, 1998.

Arnold, Sam'l P. *Eating Up the Santa Fe Trail.* Niwot, CO: University Press of Colorado, 1990.

Barry, Louise. *The Beginning of the West: Annals of the Kansas Gateway to the American West, 1540–1854.* Topeka: Kansas State Historical Society, 1972.

Baxter, John O. *Las Carneradas: Sheep Trade in New Mexico, 1700–1860.* Albuquerque: University of New Mexico Press, 1987.

Beck, Warren A. *New Mexico: A History of Four Centuries.* Norman: University of Oklahoma Press, 1962.

Beck, Warren A., and Ynez D. Haase. *Historical Atlas of New Mexico.* Norman: University of Oklahoma Press, 1969.

Bolton, Herbert Eugene. *Coronado: Knight of Pueblos and Plains.* Albuquerque: University of New Mexico Press, 1949.

———. *Pageant in the Wilderness: The Story of the Escalante Expedition to the Interior Basin, 1776.* Salt Lake City: Utah State Historical Society, 1951.

Boyd, E. *Popular Arts of Spanish New Mexico.* Santa Fe: Museum of New Mexico Press, 1974.

Boyle, Susan Calafate. *Comerciantes, Arrieros, y Peones: The Hispanos and the Santa Fe Trade.* Santa Fe, NM: Southwest Cultural Resources Center, 1994.

Cabeza de Vaca, Fabiola. *We Fed Them Cactus.* Albuquerque: University of New Mexico Press, 1954.

Carroll, H. Bailey, and J. Villasana Haggard, trans. *Three New Mexico Chronicles.* Albuquerque: Quivira Society, 1942.

Chávez, Fray Angélico. *But Time and Chance: The Story of Padre Martínez of Taos, 1793–1867.* Santa Fe, NM: The Sunstone Press, 1981.

———. *My Penitente Land: Reflections on Spanish New Mexico.* 1974. Reprint, Santa Fe: Museum of New Mexico Press, 1993.

————. *Origins of New Mexico Families: A Genealogy of the Spanish Colonial Period.* 1954. Revised Edition, Santa Fe: Museum of New Mexico Press, 1992.

Chávez, Fray Angélico, and Ted J. Warner, trans. and eds. *The Domínquez-Escalante Journal: Their Expedition Through Colorado, Utah, Arizona, and New Mexico in 1776.* Provo, Utah: Brigham Young University Press, 1976.

Chávez, Fray Angélico, and Thomas E. Chávez. *Wake for a Fat Vicar: Father Juan Felipe Ortiz, Archbishop Lamy, and the New Mexican Catholic Church in the Middle of the Nineteenth Century.* Albuquerque: LPD Press, 2004.

Chávez, Thomas E. *An Illustrated History of New Mexico.* 1992. Reprint, Albuquerque: University of New Mexico Press, 2003.

————. *Manuel Alvarez, 1794–1856: A Southwestern Biography.* Niwot, CO: University Press of Colorado, 1990.

————. *Quest for Quivira: Spanish Explorers on the Great Plains, 1540–1821.* Tucson, AZ: Southwest Parks Association, 1992.

Chilton, Lance, et. al. *New Mexico: A New Guide to the Colorful State.* Albuquerque: University of New Mexico Press, 1984.

Christiansen, Paige W., and Frank E. Kottlowski, eds. *New Mexico: A Mosaic of Science and History.* Socorro, NM: New Mexico Institute of Mining and Technology, 1963.

Church, Peggy Pond. *The House at Otowi Bridge: The Story of Edith Warner and Los Alamos.* 1959. Reprint, Albuquerque, University of New Mexico Press, 1960.

Clark, Ira G. *Water in New Mexico: A History of its Management and Use.* Albuquerque: University of New Mexico Press, 1987.

Cleaveland, Agnes Morley. *No Life for a Lady.* Boston: Houghton Mifflin Co., 1941.

Cleland, Robert Glass. *This Reckless Breed of Men.* New York: Knopf, 1950.

Colligan, John B. *The Juan Páez Hurtado Expedition of 1695: Fraud in Recruiting Colonists for New Mexico.* Albuquerque: University of New Mexico Press, 1995.

Conron, John P. *Socorro, a Historic Survey.* Albuquerque: University of New Mexico Press, 1980.

Cook, Mary J. Straw. *Loretto: The Sisters and Their Santa Fe Chapel.* Santa Fe: Museum of New Mexico Press, 2002.

Cordell, Linda. *Archaeology of the Southwest.* 1984. Reprint, New York: Academic Press, Inc., 1997.

DeBuys, William. *Enchantment and Exploitation: The Life and Times of a New Mexico Mountain Range.* Albuquerque: University of New Mexico Press, 1985.

DeMark, Judith Boyce. *Essays in Twentieth-Century New Mexico History.* Albuquerque: University of New Mexico Press, 1994.

Dozier, Edward P. *The Pueblo Indians of North America.* New York: Holt, Rinehart and Winston, 1970.

Dutton, Bertha P. *Indians of New Mexico: Land of Enchantment.* Santa Fe, NM: Tourist Division, Department of Development, 1973.

Ebright, Malcolm. *Land Grants and Lawsuits in Northern New Mexico.* Albuquerque: University of New Mexico Press, 1994.

Ellis, Bruce. *Bishop Lamy's Santa Fe Cathedral with Records of the Spanish Church (Parroquia) and Convent Formerly on the Site.* Albuquerque: University of New Mexico Press, 1985.

Ellis, Richard N., ed. *New Mexico Historic Documents.* Albuquerque: University of New Mexico Press, 1975.

———, ed. *New Mexico, Past and Present: A Historical Reader.* Albuquerque: University of New Mexico Press, 1971.

Espinosa, Aurelio M. *The Folklore of Spain in the American Southwest: Traditional Spanish Folk Literature in Northern New Mexico and Southern Colorado.* Edited by J. Manuel Espinosa. Norman: University of Oklahoma Press, 1985.

Espinosa, J. Manuel. *Crusaders of the Rio Grande: The Story of Don Diego de Vargas and the Reconquest and Refounding of New Mexico*. Chicago: Institute of Jesuit History, 1942.

Etulain, Richard W., ed. *Contemporary New Mexico, 1940–1990*. Albuquerque: University of New Mexico Press, 1994.

Flint, Richard, and Shirley Cushing Flint, eds. *The Coronado Expedition from the Distance of 460 Years*. Albuquerque: University of New Mexico Press, 2003.

Forbes, Jack D. *Apache, Navaho, and Spaniard*. Norman: University of Oklahoma Press, 1960.

Fowler, Don D. *A Laboratory for Anthropology: Science and Romanticism in the American Southwest, 1846–1930*. Albuquerque: University of New Mexico Press, 2000.

Frazer, Robert W. *Forts of the West*. Norman: University of Oklahoma Press, 1965.

Garbarino, Merwyn S. *Native American Heritage*. Boston: Little, Brown, 1976.

García, F. Chris, and Paul L. Hain, eds. *New Mexico Government*. Albuquerque: University of New Mexico Press, 1994.

García, Nasario, trans. and ed. *Abuelitos: Stories of the Río Puerco Valley*. Albuquerque: University of New Mexico Press, 1992.

———. *Más Antes: Hispanic Folklore of the Río Puerco Valley*. Santa Fe: Museum of New Mexico Press, 1997.

———. *Recuerdos de los Viejitos: Tales of the Río Puerco*. Albuquerque: University of New Mexico Press, 1987.

Garrard, Lewis H. *Wah-to-yah and the Taos Trail*. 1850. Reprint, Norman: University of New Mexico Press, 1974.

Gell-Mann, Murray. *The Quark and the Jaguar: Adventures in the Simple and the Complex*. New York: W. H. Freeman and Company, 1994.

Gomez, Art, and Lucian Niemeyer. *New Mexico: Images of a Land and Its People*. Albuquerque: University of New Mexico Press, 2004.

Gregg, Josiah. *Commerce of the Prairies.* 1844. Reprint, Edited by Max L. Moorhead, Norman: University of Oklahoma Press, 1974.

Hackett, Charles W. *Revolt of the Pueblo Indians of New Mexico and Otermin's Attempted Reconquest, 1680–1682.* 2 vols. 2nd edition. Albuquerque: University of New Mexico Press, 1970.

Hammond, George P., and Agapito Rey. *Don Juan de Oñate, Colonizer of New Mexico, 1595–1628.* 2 vols. Albuquerque: University of New Mexico Press, 1953.

———. *The Rediscovery of New Mexico, 1580–1594.* Albuquerque: University of New Mexico Press, 1966.

Hester, James L. *Early Navajo Migrations and Acculturations in the Southwest.* Santa Fe: Museum of New Mexico Press, 1962.

Hewett, Edgar L. *The Chaco Canyon and Its Monuments.* Albuquerque: University of New Mexico Press, 1936.

———. *Pajarito Plateau and Its Ancient People.* Albuquerque: University of New Mexico and School of American Research, 1938.

Holmes, Jack E. *Politics in New Mexico.* Albuquerque: University of New Mexico Press, 1967.

Hordes, Stanley. *To the End of the Earth: A History of the Crypto-Jews of New Mexico.* New York: Columbia University Press, 2005.

Horgan, Paul. *Lamy of Santa Fe: His Life and Times.* New York: Farrar, Straus and Giroux, 1975.

———. *The Great River: The Rio Grande in North American History.* New York: Holt, Rinehart, 1954.

Hotz, Gottfried. *The Segesser Hide Paintings: Masterpieces Depicting Spanish Colonial New Mexico.* 1970. Reprint, Santa Fe: Museum of New Mexico Press, 1991.

Jaehn, Tomas, comp. and ed. *Jewish Pioneers of New Mexico.* Santa Fe: Museum of New Mexico Press, 2003.

Jenkins, Myra Ellen, and Albert H. Schroeder. *A Brief History of New Mexico.* Albuquerque: University of New Mexico Press, 1974.

Jones, Oakah L. *Nueva Vizcaya: Heartland of the Spanish Frontier.* Albuquerque: University of New Mexico Press, 1998.

Julyan, Robert. *The Place Names of New Mexico.* Revised Edition, Albuquerque: University of New Mexico Press, 1998.

Keleher, William A. *Turmoil in New Mexico, 1836–1868.* Santa Fe: The Rydal Press, 1952.

Kenner, Charles L. *A History of New Mexican–Plains Indian Relations.* Norman: University of Oklahoma Press, 1969.

Kern, Robert, ed. *Labor in New Mexico: Unions, Strikes, and Social History Since 1881.* Albuquerque: University of New Mexico Press, 1983.

Kessell, John L. *Kiva, Cross, and Crown: The Pecos Indians and New Mexico, 1540–1840.* Washington: U.S. Government Printing Office, 1979.

———. *Spain in the Southwest: A Narrative History of Colonial New Mexico, Arizona, Texas, and California.* Norman: University of Oklahoma Press, 2002.

———. *The Journals of Don Diego de Vargas, New Mexico, 1691–1704.* 6 vols. Albuquerque: University of New Mexico Press, 1989–2002.

La Farge, Oliver. *Behind the Mountains.* 1956. Reprint, North Hollywood: Charles Publishing, 1994.

———. *Santa Fe: The Autobiography of a Southwestern Town.* 1959. Reprint, Norman: University of Oklahoma Press, 1970.

Lamar, Howard Roberts. *The Far Southwest: A Territorial History, 1846–1912.* New Haven: Yale University Press, 1966.

Lange, Charles H., and Carroll L. Riley. *Bandelier: The Life and Adventures of Adolf Bandelier.* Salt Lake City: University of Utah Press, 1996.

Larson, Robert L. *New Mexico's Quest for Statehood, 1846–1912.* Albuquerque: University of New Mexico Press, 1968.

Lavender, David. *Bent's Fort.* 1954. Reprint, Lincoln: Bison/University of Nebraska Press, 1972.

Los Alamos Historical Society. *Los Alamos: Beginning of an Era, 1943–1945*. 1967. Reprint, Los Alamos: Los Alamos Historical Society, 1992.

Lovato, Andrew Leo. *Santa Fe Hispanic Culture: Preserving Identity in a Tourist Town*. Albuquerque: University of New Mexico Press, 2004.

McNitt, Frank. *Navajo Wars: Military Campaigns, Slave Raids and Reprisals*. Albuquerque: University of New Mexico Press, 1971.

———. *Richard Wetherill: Anasazi: Pioneer Explorer of Ancient Ruins in the American Southwest*. 1957. Reprint, Albuquerque: University of New Mexico Press, 1966.

Meinig, D. W. *Southwest: Three People in Geographic Change, 1600–1970*. New York: Oxford University Press, 1971.

Melzer, Richard. *Ernie Pyle in the American Southwest*. Santa Fe, NM: The Sunstone Press, 1996.

Meyer, Michael C. *Water in the Hispanic Southwest*. Tucson: University of Arizona Press, 1984.

Miller, Darlis A. *The California Column in New Mexico*. Albuquerque: University of New Mexico Press, 1982.

Moorhead, Max L. *The Apache Frontier: Jacobo de Ugarte and Spanish-Indian Relations in Northern New Spain, 1769–1791*. Norman: University of Oklahoma Press, 1968.

———. *New Mexico's Royal Road: Trade and Travel of the Chihuahua Trail*. Norman: University of Oklahoma Press, 1954.

Muehlberger, William R., Sally J. Muehlberger, and L. Greer Price. *High Plains of Northeastern New Mexico: A Guide to Geology and Culture*. Socorro, NM: New Mexico Bureau of Geology and Mineral Resources, 2005.

Myrick, David F. *New Mexico's Railroads: A Historical Survey*. Golden, CO: Colorado Railroad Museum, 1970.

National Park Service and the Bureau of Land Management. *El Camino Real de Tierra Adentro Comprehensive Management Plan/Final Environment Impact Statement*. Washington: U.S. Department of the Interior, 2002.

New Mexico State Planning Office (White, Koch, Kelly, and McCarthy, Attorneys at Law). *Land Title Study*. Santa Fe: New Mexico State Planning Office, 1971.

Noble, David Grant. *Ancient Ruins of the Southwest: An Archaeological Guide*. Flagstaff: Northland Publishing, 2000.

Noyes, Stanley. *Los Comanches: The Horse People, 1751–1845*. Albuquerque: University of New Mexico Press, 1993.

Palmer, Gabrielle G., ed. *El Camino Real de Tierra Adentro*. Santa Fe, NM: Bureau of Land Management, 1993.

Pérez de Villagrá, Gaspar. *Historia de la Nueva México*. 1610. Edited and Translated by Miguel Encinias, Alfred Rodríquez, and Joseph P. Sánchez. Albuquerque: University of New Mexico Press, 1992.

Proceedings of the Sesquicentennial Symposium, 1846–1996, Commemorating New Mexico's Year of Destiny, 1846–1996. Las Cruces: Doña Ana County Historical Society and Academy for Learning in Retirement, 1996.

Riley, Glenda, and Richard W. Etulain, eds. *Wild Women of the Old West*. Golden, CO: Fulcrum Publishing, 2003.

Roberts, Calvin A. *Our New Mexico: A Twentieth Century History*. Albuquerque: University of New Mexico Press, 2005.

Sando, Joe S. *Pueblo Nations: Eight Centuries of Pueblo Indian History*. Santa Fe, NM: Clear Light Publishers, 1992.

Scholes, France V. *Church and State in New Mexico, 1610–1650*. Albuquerque: Historical Society of New Mexico, 1937.

———. *Troublous Times in New Mexico, 1659–1670*. Albuquerque: Historical Society of New Mexico, 1942.

Schroeder, Albert H., ed. *The Changing Ways of Southwestern Indians: A Historical Perspective*. Glorieta, NM: Rio Grande Press, 1973.

Simmons, Marc. *Albuquerque: A Narrative History*. Albuquerque: University of New Mexico Press, 1982.

———. *The Last Conquistador: Juan de Oñate and the Settling of the Far Southwest*. Norman: University of Oklahoma Press, 1991.

———. *The Little Lion of the Southwest.* Athens, OH: Swallow Press/Ohio University Press, 1973.

———. *New Mexico: An Interpretive History.* Albuquerque: University of New Mexico Press, 1977.

———. *Spanish Government in New Mexico.* Albuquerque: University of New Mexico Press, 1968.

Snow, David H. *New Mexico's First Colonists: The 1597–1600 Enlistments for New Mexico under Juan de Oñate, Adelante and Gobernador.* Albuquerque: Hispanic Genealogical Research Center of New Mexico, 1996.

Sonnichsen, C. L. *The Mescalero Apaches.* Norman: University of Oklahoma Press, 1958.

Spidle, Jake. *Doctors of Medicine in New Mexico: A History of Health and Medical Practice, 1886–1986.* Albuquerque: University of New Mexico Press, 1986.

Steele, Thomas J., SJ, ed. and trans. *Archbishop Lamy: In His Own Words.* Albuquerque: LPD Press, 2000.

Stark, Anne B. *Music of the Spanish Folk Plays in New Mexico.* Santa Fe: Museum of New Mexico Press, 2000.

Szasz, Ferenc. *The Day the Sun Rose Twice: The Story of the Trinity Site Nuclear Explosion, July 16, 1945.* Albuquerque: University of New Mexico Press, 1984.

Taylor, Morris F. *First Mail West: Stagecoach Lines on the Santa Fe Trail.* Albuquerque: University of New Mexico Press, 1971.

Thomas, Alfred Barnaby, ed. and trans. *After Coronado: Spanish Exploration Northeast of New Mexico, 1696–1727: Documents from the Archives of Spain, Mexico, and New Mexico.* Norman: University of Oklahoma Press, 1935.

———. *Forgotten Frontiers: A Study of the Spanish Indian Policy of Don Juan Bautista de Anza, Governor of New Mexico, 1777–1787: From the Original Documents in the Archives of Spain, Mexico, and New Mexico.* 1932. Reprint, Norman: University of Oklahoma Press, 1969.

Tiller, Veronica E. Velarde. *The Jicarilla Apache Tribe: A History.* Lincoln: University of Nebraska Press, 1992

Weber, David J. *The Mexican Frontier, 1821–1846: The American Southwest under Mexico.* Albuquerque: University of New Mexico Press, 1982.

———. *The Spanish Frontier in North America.* New Haven: Yale University Press, 1992.

———. *The Taos Trappers: The Fur Trade in the Far Southwest, 1540–1846.* Norman: University of Oklahoma Press, 1971.

Weigle, Marta. *Brothers of Light, Brothers of Blood: The Penitentes of the Southwest.* Albuquerque: University of New Mexico Press, 1970.

Weigle, Marta, and Peter White. *The Lore of New Mexico.* Albuquerque: University of New Mexico Press, 1988.

Westphall, Victor. *Mercedes Reales: Hispanic Land Grants of the Upper Rio Grande Region.* Albuquerque: University of New Mexico Press, 1983.

———. *The Public Domain in New Mexico, 1854–1891.* Albuquerque: University of New Mexico Press, 1965.

White, Robert R., ed. *The Taos Society of Artists.* Albuquerque: University of New Mexico Press, 1983.

Wilson, John P. *Merchants, Guns and Money: The Story of Lincoln County and Its Wars.* Santa Fe: Museum of New Mexico Press, 1987.

NOVELS

Anaya, Rudolfo A. *Bless Me, Ultima.* 1972. Reprint, New York: Warner Books, 1999.

Bandelier, Adolph F. *The Delight Makers: A Novel of Prehistoric Pueblo Indians.* 1980. Reprint, New York: Harcourt Brace, 1971.

Bradford, Richard. *Red Sky at Morning*. 1968. Reprint, New York: Harper and Row, 1986.

Candelaria, Nash. *Not by the Sword*. Ypsilanti, MI: Bilingual Press/Editorial Bilingue, 1982.

Cather, Willa. *Death Comes for the Archbishop*. 1927. Reprint, New York: Vintage Books, 1990.

Chávez, Fray Angélico. *The Lady from Toledo: An Historical Novel of Santa Fe*. 1960. Reprint, Santa Fe, NM: Friends of the Palace Press, 1993.

Christie, Pamela. *The King's Lizard: A Tale of Murder and Deception in Old Santa Fe*. Santa Fe, NM: Lone Butte Press, 2004.

Crawford, Stanley. *Mayordomo: Chronicle of an Acequia in Northern New Mexico*. 1988. Reprint, Albuquerque: University of New Mexico Press, 1998.

Encinias, Miguel. *Two Lives for Oñate*. Albuquerque: University of New Mexico Press, 1997.

Garrigues, Eduardo. *Al Oeste de Babilonia*. 1999. Translated by Nasario García and published in English as *West of Babylon: A Novel*. Albuquerque: University of New Mexico Press, 2002.

Horgan, Paul. *The Centuries of Santa Fe*. 1956. Reprint, Albuquerque: University of New Mexico Press, 1994.

La Farge, Oliver. *Laughing Boy*. 1929. Reprint, Boston: Mariner Books, 2004.

Laughlin, Ruth. *The Wind Leaves No Shadow*. 1948. Reprint, Caldwell, ID: Caxton Printers, 1992.

Momaday, N. Scott. *House Made of Dawn*. 1968. Reprint, New York: Perennial Classics, 1999.

Nichols, John. *The Milagro Beanfield War*. 1974. Reprint, New York: Henry Holt, 1994.

O'Meara, Walter. *The Spanish Bride*. 1954. Reprint, Santa Fe, NM: Friends of the Palace Press, 1990.

Otis, Raymond. *Miguel of the Bright Mountain*. 1936. Reprint, Albuquerque: University of New Mexico Press, 1977.

Rhodes, Eugene Manlove. *Pasó Por Aquí*. Norman: University of Oklahoma Press, 1973.

Romero, Orlando. *Nambe—Year One*. Berkeley, CA: Tonatiuh-Quinto Sol International, 1976.

Savage, Les, Jr. *The Royal City*. 1956. Reprint, Santa Fe: Friends of the Palace Press, 1988.

Waters, Frank. *The Man Who Killed the Deer*. 1942, Reprint, New York: Pocket Books, 1971.

Books for Youth

Alter, Judy. *The Santa Fe Trail*. New York: Children's Press, 1998.

Burroughs, Jean M. *Children of Destiny: True Adventures of Three Cultures*. Santa Fe, NM: Sunstone Press, 1975.

Carson, William C. *Peter Becomes a Trail Man: The Story of a Boy's Journey on the Santa Fe Trail*. Albuquerque: University of New Mexico Press, 2002.

Dewey, Jennifer Owings. *Zozobra: The Story of Old Man Gloom*. Albuquerque: University of New Mexico Press, 2004.

Ebinger, Virginia Nylander. *Niñez: Spanish Songs, Games, and Stories of Childhood*. Santa Fe, NM: Sunstone Press, 1993.

La Farge, Oliver. *The Mother Ditch*. 1954. Reprint, Santa Fe: Sunstone Press, 1983.

Roberts, Calvin. *Our New Mexico: A Twentieth Century History*. Albuquerque: University of New Mexico Press, 2005.

Simmons, Marc. *José's Buffalo Hunt: A True Story from History*. Albuquerque: University of New Mexico Press, 2003.

———. *New Mexico!* 1983. Reprint, Albuquerque: University of New Mexico Press, 2004.

Torres, Eliseo "Cheo," and Timothy Sawyer, Jr. *Stories of Mexico's Independence Days and Other Bilingual Children's Fables.* Albuquerque: University of New Mexico Press, 2005.

Tripp, Valarie. *The Books about Josephina.* Vols. 1–6. Middleton, WI: Pleasant Company Publications, 1997–98.

Index

🙰

Page numbers in *italics* indicate illustrations.